Tx 512-472-8783

# PREACHING THE GOSPEL IN THE WAY OF LIFE

## WITNESS LEE

*Living Stream Ministry*
Anaheim, CA

First Edition, January 2002.

ISBN 0-7363-1539-X

Published by

*Living Stream Ministry*
2431 W. La Palma Ave., Anaheim, CA 92801 U.S.A.
P. O. Box 2121, Anaheim, CA 92814 U.S.A.

*Printed in the United States of America*

02   03   04   05   06   07   08   /   10   9   8   7   6   5   4   3   2   1

# CONTENTS

# PREFACE

This book is composed of messages given by Brother Witness Lee in Los Angeles, California in the Spring of 1965. Chapters One through Three were spoken in preparation for a gospel meeting, Chapter Four is the message given in the gospel meeting, and Chapters Five and Six are the fellowship given to the newly saved believers. The remainder of the book is general fellowship on the gospel. These messages were not reviewed by the speaker.

# CHAPTER ONE

# HOW TO HELP PEOPLE TO BE SAVED

Scripture Reading: Acts 10:43; Eph. 1:7; Acts 13:38-39; John 3:16, 36; 5:24; 6:47; Rom. 10:9-10, 13; Acts 16:31

## BEARING THE BURDEN FOR PEOPLE'S SOULS WITH A PRAYING SPIRIT

In preaching the gospel two matters are very important. First, we have to pray. We always need to bear the burden for people's souls with a praying spirit. This not only means that we have to spend time to pray; even more it means that we have to always bear the burden in our praying spirit, looking to the Lord and touching the throne of authority, that the Lord will move in the hearts of those people for whom we have been praying. We must pray in this way, in a continuous way, and in a claiming way, to claim these souls for the Lord's testimony.

## EXERCISING FAITH TO PARTICIPATE IN THE POWER THAT IS UPON THE BODY

Second, we must learn how to exercise faith to participate in the power that is upon the Body, to experience the baptism of the Holy Spirit, which already has been accomplished upon the Body. The principle of both the spiritual life and the spiritual work is the principle of faith, not of sight or appearance. We must learn to walk and to work by faith, not by sight, appearance, or feeling. To seek feeling, sight, or appearance means that more or less we have an evil heart of unbelief, even an evil heart of disbelief. We have to honor the Lord by taking what He has told us in His Word. This is living faith.

Never pay attention to your feeling, to appearance, to sight, or to any kind of circumstances.

## Believing without Any Feeling or Natural Seeing

We need to learn the lesson of faith, to believe that God is with us. We have to believe "in the dark," without any feeling (2 Cor. 5:7). In the ancient time, the priests who served the Lord in the outer court used their sight. Under the light of the sun they could see the heavens, the earth, and many things and persons. In the Holy Place, however, there was only the light of the lampstand, which was not as strong as the sun. Enclosed within the Holy Place, the priests could not see the heavens, the earth, and all the surroundings, as they could in the outer court. Then when they came into the Holy of Holies, there was no light at all. The ark was there "in the dark." However, the presence of the Lord was not in the outer court or in the Holy Place; it was in the Holy of Holies. Here there was no physical light but the Shekinah light, the Shekinah glory of God; here there was not the created light but the uncreated light.

When we were young in the Lord, even childish, the Lord sympathized with us and gave us an "open heaven." When some people are baptized, they receive the outpouring of the Holy Spirit. They may say, "Oh, I can almost not take it! The heavens are so open to me that I have to dance, even dance in the air and not on the ground." I know this because I have had many of these experiences. However, children are just children. These experiences are for the young ones. Do not despise this, because it is good, but it is something in the outer court. The Lord will bring us on from the outer court to exercise a little faith in the Holy Place. Eventually He has to bring us into the Holy of Holies where we exercise our faith to the uttermost. There we have to forget about our physical eyes and all the senses of our physical body. We also have to forget about the feeling of our soulish life. In the Holy of Holies we can see nothing naturally; we are "in the dark." In the spirit, though, we see the Shekinah glory of God. This is the meaning of faith.

## The Bible Being a Will

We Christians are strange. We believe and hold on to some things in the Scriptures without any feeling, but we do not believe in other things in the Scriptures; we will not hold on to them until we have the feeling. Recently I asked a brother, "Brother, do you know that you have been saved?" He said he did, so I asked, "How do you know?" He replied, "Because the Scriptures tell me." This is right.

The Bible consists of the Old Testament and the New Testament. Many Christians do not know the right meaning of the word *testament*. *Testament* is not a synonym of the word *covenant*. Using our human words, a covenant is an agreement, a contract, and a testament is a will. A will is not merely an agreement. In a covenant, an agreement or contract, there may be certain promises, promising something will be done for you. In a will, however, everything is completed and ready for you. The Bible is a will in our hands. It is not a book of teaching or even of promises; it is book containing a will. In it there are thousands of items telling us that everything is ready for us. Christ was incarnated, lived on this earth, was crucified and resurrected, ascended, was seated and enthroned, and has descended as the Spirit. Everything is finished. What does it mean that Christ is sitting in the heavens? It means that everything is accomplished, finished, and ready, waiting for us to enjoy. A will goes into effect at the time the giver dies. Without the death of the giver, the will is not good. After the death of the giver, however, the will is in effect. The Giver of this will has died already, and He is living in the heavens as the Executor of His will.

What we go to tell the sinners are the items of this testament, this will. What is the preaching of the gospel? The preaching of the gospel is the proclaiming of the items of this will. When we go to a sinner, we must help him to realize that he is a sinner. Then we can read the will to him. We can first read the item in the will that tells us that our sins have been put on Jesus, that He has borne our sins on the cross. Second, we read the item that says that due to Christ's redemption our sins have been forgiven. Then we read the item that says there is the remission of our sins. It is not that God will forgive us but that, according to the will, God has forgiven us already. Likewise, the remission of sins is here already.

## Believing That the Power from on High Is upon the Body, of Which We Are Members

In this will there is an item that says Christ has poured down His Spirit upon the Body. He has already accomplished the baptism of the Spirit upon the Body. Now, we have become members of the Body. As long as we are identified with the Body, what has been accomplished upon the Body is our portion already. The baptism of the Holy Spirit was accomplished upon the Body nearly two thousand years ago. This is already accomplished. Today we have to exercise our faith to take it. If we do not believe this, we cannot be powerful and prevailing to preach the gospel.

Besides the bearing away of our sins, the forgiveness of sins, and the remissions of sins, there is another item in this will telling us that Christ has ascended to the throne and poured out the Spirit upon His Body. Today the power from on high is on the Body, and we have been baptized into the Body. We are identified with the Body, we are a part of the Body, so we have the ground, the right, the entitlement to claim, take, and share this portion. However, we may not believe it. We may doubt it a little. When we do not believe it, we do not have the power to preach the first item of the will, concerning redemption, because the enemy who occupies the sinners still occupies us. If we still do not believe the Word in a full way, how can we help people to believe something in the will? We have to know the subtlety of the enemy. If we are going to preach any item from this will, we have to believe all the items in it. If we believe every item mentioned in this will, have no doubt, and do not care about our feeling, then when we come to someone, we have the impact, because Satan has been chased away from us.

When I was young, I was helped by the Lord to believe in Him, His Word, and His accomplished facts in this way. Then I did the work of preaching. Many times, though, when I was telling people they had to believe that the Lord Jesus died for them, within me was the accusation that I did not believe that the Lord Jesus has baptized the church. I could not fool the enemy. The evil spirit is very alert. If we have such a weakness, he will always hit this weakness. Therefore, we have to deal with this matter. If we are going to preach any item of this will, we have to believe all the items of this will.

Here we have a vital matter, that is, that we have to believe that the power from on high has been put on the Body and that now we are a part, a member, of the Body. We have to believe in this, take this ground, and not pay attention to the feeling, the manifestation. If we pay attention to the feeling, this means that unbelief and disbelief are within us. That is evil. On the other hand, of course, we should not be sloppy or slothful. We have to exercise our spirit, even exercise our will in the spirit, to believe what we are told in this will. This kind of believing, this kind of faith, honors the Giver of the will. We have to exercise our spirit and our will to take the word and reject our feeling. Even if a feeling comes to us, we reject it. We do not care about that feeling, and we can tell the enemy, "I do not care even a little about feeling. If I do not have even a little feeling, I still have the full assurance that the baptism of the Spirit is mine, because it is accomplished on the Body, and I am identified with the Body." If we do this, we will see the result. However, there is no need to pay attention even to the result. Rather, we must learn to walk in faith, to act in faith in the Holy of Holies, "in the dark," without any natural light but with the divine light in our spirit. Learn to exercise your faith in this way.

## HOW TO HELP PEOPLE TO BE SAVED

Now we come to a very important point—how to help people to be saved. We cannot save people, but we can help people to be saved. Only the Lord Himself can save people, but we can help people to receive the Lord, to accept the Lord and accept salvation. It is needless to say that we must have a real love and concern toward the sinners; if we do not have love and concern for sinners, our work is over. Suppose then, that we do have this love, this concern, and we pray for sinners and exercise our faith to participate in the power from on high, not paying attention to our feeling. Then we have to learn some techniques of how to help people.

## Not Being Tempted to Make People Clear but Rather Leading Them to Pray

First, we should not talk too much to the sinners, the unbelievers. We should speak with them in a very brief way. In addition, we should not try to make them clear. Many times, the more people are clear, the more they will not believe. Many times we are tempted to think that if we can make someone clear, he surely will believe. Rather, the more we make someone clear, the more he will not believe. Keep this principle: Do not try to make people clear. If we try to make people clear, we are doing the work of Satan, as he did in the garden when he said of the fruit of the tree of knowledge, "In the day you eat of it your eyes will be opened" (Gen. 3:5). He told Eve that she would be clear and would know many things. Immediately after Eve took that fruit, her eyes were really opened. Before this time Adam and Eve were not clear about their nakedness, but by taking that fruit their eyes were opened, they realized they were naked, and trouble came. Do not believe that if we make people clear, they will believe. Rather, everyone who is saved is a someone who is not clear. We believe "foolishly."

Someone may ask, "How can people believe without being clear?" This is a secret. They simply have to believe. When someone is favored by the Lord, he has to believe, whether or not he is clear. Many times we are not clear, but we still say, "I do not know why, but I have to believe." People may say that this is superstitious, but if so, I like to be "superstitious," the more the better. When I was young, my friends and many people came to tell me that I was just a fool. However, I told them, "I like to be a fool, the more the better. I cannot tell you what it is, but something is within me." Therefore, do not try and do not be tempted to make people clear. Simply talk with them in a brief way. After talking with them, right away ask them to pray. To pray is to "sign the deal." A good

salesman never talks too much; if he talks too much, he will
lose the deal. Simply ask them to pray.

## Helping People to Know
## That Jesus Is the Living Spirit

Then after we help people to pray, we need to help them in
several matters; otherwise, they will not be properly saved.
First, we should help them to know that to believe in Jesus
means to receive Him as the living Spirit into them. We must
stress this very much. We should tell them that Jesus today is
in the Spirit and even is the real, true, and living Spirit.
Therefore, we can open our heart and open our spirit, that is,
open our whole being to receive Him. We have to stress this
point again and again. Then those who are saved will be living
Christians. Otherwise, they will be only religious people, not
living Christians; we will merely have some religious members.
For this purpose we need to read them some verses about
Christ as our life and Christ living in us. We must help them
to know this. Do not think that we should wait until they have
been saved for a long time to tell them that Christ is life. No,
from the first day we need to tell them. I was saved in this
way. At the time I was saved, I was even told that I have been
crucified with Christ. I realized that I was finished; I was
dead with Christ and was buried already. Now it is no more I
but Christ who lives in me. I heard a complete gospel.

Do not think that this is too deep. This may be too deep
for some people in Christianity, but it is not too deep for the
sinners. Try this. Do not preach the gospel in the old way. Do
not say, "Oh, this is too deep. Half a year later we can let
Brother Lee minister to them how Christ is life to the believers." No, this is wrong. There are many deep things in the
Gospel of John, but that book is still called the gospel. The
whole book of Romans is also called the gospel. The first
chapter of Romans tells us that the whole book is the gospel
(vv. 1, 9, 15-16, cf. 16:25). We should even learn to preach the
gospel from Romans 12, telling people that they have to be
members of the Body. We must tell people definitely and thoroughly that Christ is a living Spirit today, waiting for people
to receive Him as life. Stress this matter.

### Helping People with Some Practical Verses

Following this, we have to tell people that if they are going to receive Christ as the living One, they have to make a thorough confession. They need to confess their sins. No doubt, we must tell them that their sins have been borne away by Christ and forgiven by God. However, for their experience of Christ, there is a need for them to confess all of their sins. We should help them to realize how many sins they have, how sinful they are, and help them to repent and confess their sins in a thorough way. They may ask how to confess. We can tell them that they should confess according to what they feel. There is nothing legal. They should simply contact the Lord and confess whatever they feel is sinful or dirty, the more the better.

We must also give people some practical verses from the New Testament, and sometimes from the Old Testament, to prove to them that they have really been saved. There are four main items that we have to help them to see.

### *Showing Them That Their Sins Have Been Forgiven*

First, by quoting some verses we must help them to know that their sins have been forgiven. The remission of sins has been given to them. The best verse concerning the forgiveness of sins is Acts 10:43, which says, "To this One all the prophets testify that through His name everyone who believes into Him will receive forgiveness of sins." We should read this verse to people and ask them also to read it. This is the way to point out this item of the will. In the will there is such an item telling us that if we believe in His name, our sins are forgiven; the remission of sins has been given to us. We may also use Ephesians 1:7, but Acts 10:43 is the best verse. In this way we must give people some practical verses from the New Testament to confirm them, to prove that what we have been preaching is not a theory but an item of the will.

### *Showing Them That They Are Justified by Faith*

After reading the words in the will concerning the forgiveness of sins, we should read to them about justification by faith. From the Word prove to them that they have been justified by faith. There are many such verses. I prefer Acts 13:38 and 39, which say, "Therefore let it be known to you, men, brothers, that through this One forgiveness of sins is announced to you; and from all the things from which you were not able to be justified by the law of Moses, in this One everyone who believes is justified." These two verses tell us two things, that forgiveness is announced and that justification has been given in this One, that is, in Christ. We may also use many verses from Romans 3 and Galatians 2, quoting the best verses to confirm that as long as a person believes in Jesus, he has been justified by God in Christ. This is the forgiveness of sins and justification by faith.

### Showing Them That They Have Eternal Life

Third, we should read some verses confirming that they have eternal life within them. There are many such verses, such as John 3:16 and 36, 5:24, 6:47, and others. We need these verses to confirm, to prove, that they have eternal life in them.

### Showing Them That They Have Been Saved

Besides showing people forgiveness of sins, justification by faith, and eternal life, we need to show them verses that tell them they are saved. The best verses for this are Romans 10:9 and 10, which say, "If you confess with your mouth Jesus as Lord and believe in your heart that God has raised Him from the dead, you will be saved; for with the heart there is believing unto righteousness, and with the mouth there is confession unto salvation." In addition, verse 13 says, "Whoever calls upon the name of the Lord shall be saved." We may also use Acts 16:31: "And they said, Believe on the Lord Jesus, and you shall be saved, you and your household."

We must stress these four main points from the Word: they are forgiven, they are justified, they have received eternal life, and they are saved. We can give them more, but these four items are very necessary. We cannot do too much by one contact alone. After preaching to them, we may only do the first thing, that is, help them to pray. Then the very next day we may go to contact them again to help them realize that the Lord Christ is the living Spirit. Perhaps then there will be time to help them with these practical verses. If we do not have enough time, we can leave something for the third contact. We should not try to do everything at one time.

## Helping People to Know the Body

We have seen three main items related to helping people to be saved. We must help them to pray to "close the deal"; we must help them to realize that Christ is the living Spirit, that they have to receive Him by opening their heart and their spirit; and we need to help them with some practical verses. We should also help people to know that they are saved by the Lord through the church. They have to realize their relationship to the church. From the very beginning we have to help the new believers to know the Body. They will never forget what they are impressed with at the very beginning. We have to explain to them that from this time on they need to come to the church meetings. They have to come to contact the brothers and to have fellowship with the brothers.

When someone is saved through us, we should immediately help him to realize the church life. Then we should recommend two or three brothers or sisters as their new companions in the church. This will be a great help to them. Every new believer, every new convert, will have at least two or three brothers as Christian companions. We all have to learn to help people in this way.

After a meeting for preaching the gospel, we should ask the new believers to come for three nights of follow up. In this way we can immediately give them some training. We should not think, though, that these are their meetings, so we should not come. Rather, it is our turn to come to practice. Then after this follow-up work, we can baptize them. On the following Lord's Day, we will have a good number of new believers in the Lord's table meeting. These will be the "new folks" in our family. Then we can help them to know a little bit about the church, and they will realize that the church, the Body, is their home. We should also help them to know that we do not preach the gospel individualistically; we preach the gospel in a Body way, a corporate way. From the first day they should know that this is the church preaching the gospel, not to bring people to heaven, but to bring people to the church. Then we will see the difference. We have to believe that after only two weeks they will bring many people to believe. They will function even better than we do.

## Helping the Saved Ones
## to Offer Themselves to the Lord

After we help them to this extent, we must help them to offer themselves to the Lord, to consecrate themselves. All these foregoing five items should be done within one week. This means that even before they are baptized, we have to help them with all these points.

I do not want to make anything legal, but I would beg you to learn to do this. I stand here humbly to tell you that if we all would practice this, we will see the effect. We will see the impact of the preaching. Many persons will be saved. Our meeting for preaching the gospel is only a start of the preaching. More people will follow. One fish in the sea always bites the tail of another one. If we can catch one, many will come in. We will reap the harvest. If we will do this well, every month we will bring in a good number "by the tail." However, we have to learn how to work and how to help the new ones to work. We should visit them right away to help them to work. They have now become members of the church, even "leading" members. They will take the lead more than we do because they do not have much knowledge; they only have life. We have too much knowledge. Our "head" is too big.

The Lord covers me to say this. I am looking to the Lord very much; I have been looking and still am looking to the Lord for this matter. This is the secret of the church's preaching. Do not trust any speaker. In our meeting for preaching the gospel there may be no speaker, yet the gospel will be preached. Do you believe this? I believe this, because I saw it in the past. Many persons were saved in a living way, but they did not know through which speaker. They could never say that they made their decision through a certain famous preacher. We did not have that kind of famous preacher in the

Far East, but thousands of people were saved. Rather, we had the church, the whole Body, and the exercise of every part of the Body.

## Helping People to Realize Their Need of Baptism

After helping people with the five foregoing items, we must help them to realize their need of baptism. We have to testify to them and explain to them what it means to be baptized, helping them to realize that since they have been identified with Christ, they have been crucified and are now dead. Therefore, they have to be buried. Regarding baptism, they have to exercise their faith to believe that in many cases a great blessing came down to those who were baptized. I saw people healed through baptism. Before they went into the water, they were very sick, not merely with a cold but with a chronic sickness. After baptism, however, some people have been healed. We are not superstitious concerning water baptism, but there is really something to it. There must be, because the Lord commanded us to do it. We should not take baptism as a mere ritual. We should tell people that it must be a spiritual realization.

We should also help them to know that when they are baptized, they bring all their problems with them to be buried, just as Israel brought the whole of Egypt into the Red Sea when they crossed it. It was not they who were buried there, but the whole of Egypt, including Pharaoh and his army. We should tell them that if they have any problem, even physical sickness, they take it into the water and bury it there. Do they have some besetting sin or a moral weakness? They bring it into the water. They bring everything into the water. They especially bring their pleasures into the water. In the Far East and in many other places, when someone is buried, the things they loved, their favorite things, are buried with them. In a sense, this is scriptural. When people are baptized, they bring whatever they love to be buried in the water. We must help them to realize all these matters.

### FOUR MATTERS AFTER BAPTISM

After they are baptized, we have to help them with four

matters. First, we must help them to pray in a daily and hidden way. Second, we must help them to study the Word day by day. Third, we need to help them to attend the regular meetings of the church. Fourth, we should help them to preach the gospel. They have to pray, they have to study, they have to attend the meetings, and they have to act to bring others to the next meeting for gospel preaching. They have to be the most active members in the gospel preaching of the church. If we cannot or will not work this out, we will have a failure. All the sinners who come to the first gospel meeting must be the preachers in the next gospel meeting. This does not depend as much on the Lord as it depends on us. It depends on how much we labor and in what way we work. I am sure that we will see a good result if we will work in this way.

# CHAPTER TWO

# PREACHING THE GOSPEL
# WITH CHRIST'S AUTHORITY AND
# THE LIVING WORD

Scripture Reading: Matt. 12:28-29; 28:18-19; Rom. 10:6-9, 13; 1 Cor. 12:3

Matthew 12:28 and 29 say, "But if I, by the Spirit of God, cast out the demons, then the kingdom of God has come upon you. Or how can anyone enter into the house of the strong man and plunder his goods unless he first binds the strong man? And then he will thoroughly plunder his house." Verses 18 and 19 of chapter twenty-eight say, "And Jesus came and spoke to them, saying, All authority has been given to Me in heaven and on earth. Go therefore and disciple all the nations, baptizing them into the name of the Father and of the Son and of the Holy Spirit." We need to read the word *therefore* strongly. *Therefore* refers to the fact that all authority has been given to Christ. For this cause, "therefore," we must go to disciple all the nations, to make all the nations disciples.

## CONFESSING JESUS AS LORD

Romans 10:9 says, "That if you confess with your mouth Jesus as Lord and believe in your heart that God has raised Him from the dead, you will be saved." This is to confess not only Jesus but the Lord Jesus. The mouth has to confess the Lord Jesus; it must pronounce "Lord." I have found that especially in the Western world, both in Europe and America, when people pray, they do not use the title *Lord* very much. Mostly they pray saying only, "Jesus." This is not a proper way. Whenever we say "Jesus," it is better that we add the title *Lord,* "Lord Jesus." The mouth confesses the Lord Jesus, and the heart believes in the fact that God has raised up Jesus. If we do these two things, we will be saved. Then verse 13 says, "For 'whoever calls upon the name of the Lord shall be saved.'" This is to call not only the name of Jesus but the name of "the Lord."

First Corinthians 12:3 says, "Therefore I make known to you that no one speaking in the Spirit of God says, Jesus is accursed; and no one can say, Jesus is Lord! except in the Holy Spirit." Here again, this verse stresses our saying that Jesus is the Lord. As long as a person says that Jesus is the Lord, that is a proof that the Holy Spirit is working within him. We have to help people to realize that Jesus is the Lord, and we have to help them to exercise their mouth by exercising their heart to say that Jesus is the Lord and to call Jesus the Lord.

## PREACHING NOT ONLY WITH POWER BUT WITH THE AUTHORITY OF THE HEAVENLY GOVERNMENT

We all have to realize that to preach the gospel is not merely to preach or to teach; it is to fight the battle. Matthew 12 tells us that in order to preach the gospel we have to bind the strong man. Satan is the strong man, the one who usurps all people. The whole world is now under darkness and the usurping hand of Satan. To preach the gospel to bring someone to the Lord is to spoil some goods out of the usurping hand of Satan. Therefore, we have to pray to bind the strong man Satan. For this we need not only power but also authority. We can illustrate the difference between power and authority with a policeman. Cars on the street have power, but a policeman has authority. No matter how powerful a car is, when a policeman gives an order, he has the authority over it.

Christ said, "All authority has been given to Me in heaven and on earth. Go therefore and disciple all the nations" (Matt. 28:18-19). When we go to preach the gospel, we must not only seek power from on high, but we must learn to exercise the authority of the headship and lordship of Christ. A policeman may be smaller than we are, but he has the authority because there is a government behind him. Because we cannot go against a government, we cannot go against a policeman. I have learned that in this country all the drivers are afraid of policemen. This does not mean that the policemen have the power; it means they have the authority. Many cars on the street are powerful, but when a policeman gives the signal, everyone has to stop. Authority is over power. Are we going out to preach the gospel only with power? We also have to learn to exercise authority. We are the Body of the Head, and we are under the headship, so we have the Head as the "government" backing us. We have a strong backing, that is, the Head.

## STANDING ON THE GROUND OF THE LORD'S AUTHORITY

I have the burden that we would realize what our ground is to preach the gospel. It is not merely the ground that we love sinners or that we feel that there is the need for materials for the building up of the church. All these are good, but they are not adequate. We have to take the ground that Christ has ascended to the heavens. He has been enthroned, and all authority both in heaven and on earth has been given to Him. He is the Head, and He is the Lord. We are under His headship and under His lordship. Moreover, we are the members of His Body. It is on this ground that we are sent out. In actuality we do not take the initiative; we are the sent ones. The Lord said, "All authority has been given to Me in heaven and on earth. Go therefore." We simply take the order. We are the policemen sent by the government. If we realize this, then when we go out to touch people by our preaching, we will have the assurance, the confidence, that the authority is with us.

Recently there has been a real flow and a burden among us for the gospel, and some people already have been saved. However, I sense that we are still short of something. We are short of the realization that we have to take the ground of authority. Satan is the illegal usurper. We have to announce this, and we have to proclaim this. We have to tell the whole universe that Jesus is the proper Lord, the legal owner of this universe. Today Jesus is on the throne. He is legally entitled by God as the Lord. He has received an authority that is absolutely unique both in heaven and on earth, and He has passed this authority on to us because we are His members, we are identified with Him, and we are one with Him as the Head. It is on this standing, in such a position, and taking such a ground that we go out. This is something different from mere power. When a policeman comes to us, he does not come only with power; he comes with authority. There is something great behind him. We cannot go against him because he has the authority. If our realization is to such an extent, we will have the faith and assurance that a person will be saved, and he will be spoiled out of the hand of the enemy. Let us learn this.

### TAKING THE LORD'S AUTHORITY AND ENTITLEMENT AS AN ITEM IN THE WILL

Recently the brothers and sisters have learned how to take the standing that they have been baptized with the power from on high. We have this standing because we are the members of the Body, and the Body already has been baptized. This is a reality among us in these days. However, I would point out to you something more. We have to realize that the Body of Christ has not only been baptized with the power but also entitled with the authority of Christ. We have the authority. All these matters require us to exercise our faith to realize that they are items in the will, the testament. Now we are simply discovering what the items of the will are. We have had this will for many years, yet so many items are still not clear to us. Now we are discovering all the items. In this will we have not only an item telling us that power is ours but also an item telling us that authority is ours. When we go out, we need to have this assurance, this realization. We are sent from the heavenly government, which is much greater than Washington, D.C. We are sent ones, sent from the heavenly Jerusalem. The Lord's headship is much greater than the headship of the President of the United States. In the past have you ever had such a realization when going out to contact people? We all have to realize that this is not a doctrine. We have to receive this by believing.

Now we have heard that in this will, this testament, there

is an item which says that Christ the Head, the Lord, has been entitled with the authority both in heaven and earth, and He has passed on this authority to His Body. It is on this standing with such a realization that we go out, not merely to preach the gospel but to pass on orders. This is the order of the heavenly Washington, D.C. We have to give this order not only to humans but to the demons and to the strong man, saying, "I come here in the name not only of Jesus but of the Lord Jesus. He is the Lord today. Satan, you have to take the order!" This is different from merely exercising power. This changes darkness into light and night into day. This even changes hell into heaven. There is no need for us to speak too much. We simply pass on the order. For a policeman to give a ticket does not require much work; he simply writes the ticket, and people have to take it and pay the fine. We must learn to exercise our faith as the "policemen" acting with authority.

We must learn these matters from the very beginning of our preaching of the gospel. If the Lord is willing, we will advance step by step. This is why I am speaking these things. I am truly burdened for this. I have the burden to pass on as much as I can, as much as I have learned about all the matters of the Lord's service. In our preaching there is the need that we all realize that we can exercise authority. I know what I am speaking about. Twenty years ago I did much preaching. Whenever I preached, I took the standing that I was a sent one, sent not only by the "lowly Jesus" but by the Lord Jesus. I could say, "I am a sent one in this universe, and I come with authority. Maybe you do not know this, but the devil who is in you knows. He knows that now here is one with the authority to deal with him." I could say to the devil, "Yes, I am your authority. You have to take my order. Leave this man and get out."

This makes a difference. Many times when I stood up on the platform I dared not to stand up in the realization that I could speak something. Rather, I stood in the realization that I am a sent one passing on the orders. Learn to exercise your faith in this way. Do not pay attention to feelings or to manifestations. To pay our attention to feelings and manifestations proves that we have an evil heart of unbelief. We have the will, the testament. Is this not good enough? If this is good enough, then there is no need to have a feeling, and there is no need to seek the manifestations. Simply take it and believe. The manifestations are in the hand of the Lord. We will see many wonderful things, but we should never pay attention to those things. The more we pay attention to those things, the more we will frustrate and be frustrated. As I pointed out in the previous message, the people sojourning in the outer court had many signs as manifestations, but those who served in the Holy of Holies had no signs. Rather, they had the Shekinah glory of the Lord. That was a matter of faith. Always keep the principle of working, walking, and doing things in faith not by sight. Take the item in the will that Christ has been entitled and that we are authorized. Now we go out on this standing.

### EXERCISING AUTHORITY TOWARD DEMONS
### AND NOT TOWARD PEOPLE

I have noticed that the attitude of policemen in this country is always good. I have been in this country at least twice before, and now I have been here for more than three years. I never saw a policeman in this country who was not humble, polite, meek, and lovely. However, behind this loveliness there is the authority. We should exercise the Lord's authority to deal with the demons, not with people. Rather, we have to exercise love, humility, kindness, and loveliness to deal with people. In our heart and in our realization we do say, "I am here with authority," but in our attitude with people we have to be very nice. We should not say to them, "I am one sent from the heavenly Jerusalem." This is wrong. The humbler, the nicer, and the kinder we are, the better.

To the devil and the demons we are not polite; we are very strong. However, to people we have to be kind. If we are too strong toward people, we will be utilized by the enemy. We must learn the subtle wiles of the enemy and learn how to deal with the situation. We should be strong with the enemy but kind with people.

## SPEAKING THE WORD AS THE LIVING SPIRIT

Romans 10:6 through 8 says, "But the righteousness which is out of faith speaks in this way, 'Do not say in your heart, Who will ascend into heaven?' that is, to bring Christ down; or, 'Who will descend into the abyss?' that is, to bring Christ up from the dead. But what does it say? 'The word is near you, in your mouth and in your heart,' that is, the word of the faith which we proclaim." Verses 6 and 7 speak of Christ, but in verse 8 the subject changes to "the word." The word that we preach is the word in the preacher's mouth, but here it says that the word that we preach is in the mouth of the listener, and not only is it in his mouth but also in his heart. What is this word? Is this merely a doctrine? We have to realize that the word mentioned here is the very Spirit. If we compare this verse to John 6:63, we can see that the word that the Lord speaks is spirit and life. If the word spoken by the Lord were not spirit, how could it enter into the heart of the listeners? This is the reason that while we are preaching the word in a living way, this living word becomes the Spirit in the hearts of the listeners. We can never separate the Lord's word from the Spirit. The Spirit and the word are always two in one. While we are speaking the word, the Holy Spirit mingles Himself with the word. Then when the word arrives in the hearts of the listeners, it becomes the living Spirit. If we read these few verses in Romans 10 again and again, we will realize that the word mentioned in verse 8 is not a doctrine but is something living. In the previous verses it refers to Christ, but all of a sudden in this verse it changes from Christ to the word.

Therefore, when we go to preach, we need to teach people a little, but we should not do too much teaching. We must not have the feeling that we are going to teach people. Rather, we need to have the assurance that the Lord is with us, and His living Spirit is mingled with our word. When we speak, we need the living faith that our word is a word full of the Spirit. For this reason, we have to learn not to speak the teaching of religion. We must learn to speak something about Christ, the living One. We are not ministering mere doctrines as a religion; we are ministering the living Christ to people. Of course, there is no need to declare to people that we are doing this, but we have to do it in a proper way, learning the proper way to speak. Regardless of which way we contact people, the goal, the aim, is to minister Christ to them, to bring them to realize that what they need is Christ Himself, the living One.

According to Romans 10:6 through 8, while we are preaching Christ, this kind of preaching becomes the living Spirit. We have to tell people that Christ today is all-inclusive. God is in Him, and man is in Him. We should not be afraid that they cannot understand this. Sometimes they can understand it better than we do. Recently some brothers went out to preach the gospel, telling people about the Body of Christ, God's economy, and the spirit, soul, and body. Those that they spoke to were able to receive it. This is our gospel. We must have the assurance that we are ministering Christ to people, and this Christ whom we minister to others is the all-inclusive One. Not only is He the Savior and the Redeemer, but He is also the Head, the Lord, and the One on the throne with glory and authority.

In a living way we must tell people about Christ. We should not preach the old gospel. If we preach a living Christ, the Holy Spirit will honor our preaching, and the word that we speak will become the Spirit and life to others. Our word will become the word in their heart and in their mouth. Then we can point out to them that Christ is now in their heart and in their mouth because today Christ is in the Spirit and He is the Spirit. We may give them the illustration of electricity and radio waves. When the word is spoken at the radio station, it becomes radio waves that bring the word to every part of the earth. In this sense it becomes a living word. We may tell people, "Now I am speaking in the Spirit, and the Spirit is like electricity. My word is in the Spirit, so it is in you, in your heart, as the living Spirit who also is Christ. What you need now is simply to believe in Him and say to Him, 'Lord Jesus.' If you will open your mouth to call Jesus the Lord, that means you are saved." Then we can read them 1 Corinthians 12:3, which says, "Therefore I make known to you that no one speaking in the Spirit of God says, Jesus is accursed; and no one can say, Jesus is Lord! except in the Holy Spirit." If a person says, "O Lord Jesus!", this means that the Holy Spirit is moving within him.

There is no need to go out to teach people. We simply should go to make people genuine Christians in this way. We can do it very quickly. In one minute a person can be converted. We can say, "I am speaking for Christ, and I am speaking in Christ. Now Christ is in you. Would you say, 'Lord Jesus'?" If the person does this, he will be saved. This depends on the faith that we exercise. If we go to a person and exercise our faith to such an extent, the Holy Spirit will honor it. Then we will see a real conversion, a real change in life in this man. There will be a real moving within him. That is the start of the work of the Holy Spirit. He will love the Lord, he will love the Scriptures, he will love to contact genuine Christians, and he will love to come to the meetings. This will prove that he has been saved. That he does not know much doctrine does not mean anything. We should not give him too much doctrine. Rather, we should help him in a living way.

Moreover, we should try not to argue with people, saying, "Sir, do you believe there is a God?" This opens the door for the enemy to come in to argue. It opens the door for argument and closes the door for believing. There is the fact, so there is no need to argue. There is God; there is no doubt about this. Whether or not someone acknowledges that there is a God, everyone believes deep within there is a God. Therefore, we should simply speak something in a living way about Christ. Just a few words are sufficient. Then the person we speak with will pray, "O Lord Jesus." That is good enough. Once a person calls Jesus the Lord, he is saved. We should simply tell people to call Him the Lord.

We should also help the person to realize that Christ is everywhere. Christ is omnipresent, because He is in the Spirit and He is the Spirit today. He is like electricity and like the air. Wherever we are, electricity is there and the air is there. The way to receive Him is simply by saying "Lord Jesus." Whenever a person would open his or her mouth to say "Lord Jesus," we have to say, "Hallelujah, praise the Lord! Here is a soul gained through me."

As a second step, we must tell this person that we are sinful and that we have to confess our sins. Then he will say, "Lord Jesus, I am sinful," and we can help him to see that all his sins were put on Jesus when He was crucified. We can give him the gospel in this way. Many times we have to give someone the gospel after they call on the Lord Jesus. This can be compared to bringing him to America and then showing him the things in America. We need not tell him the things about America while he is still outside of it. We can bring him to America and say, "Look, here is Los Angeles; you are right here." We must bring him into Christ and then tell him the things in Christ. Brothers, go and try to do this. These are some shortcuts for the preaching of the gospel.

## EXERCISING FAITH TO PREACH THE GOSPEL

Preaching the gospel is truly a matter of faith. Many times people say that we need love for sinners. There is no doubt that we need love and a real concern for sinners, but going out to preach the gospel is mainly a matter of faith. First, we have to believe whatever is spoken in the Word. If we do not believe, if we have even a little bit of doubt about the Scriptures, we lose the ground of faith, and the enemy, the devil and the demons, will know. Therefore, we have to exercise our faith, telling the Lord and telling the whole universe, "I believe in Jesus. I believe in the Triune God, and I believe in every word of the Scriptures." We have to exercise our faith to tell the enemy that we believe all the words in the Scriptures, so we are going out to preach the gospel with assurance, confidence, and authority.

We have to exercise in this way. We cannot be indifferent when we preach. When a policeman comes to us, he comes with a definite purpose. We must learn to exercise faith to believe that we have been saved, we have ascended to the heavens, and we have been entitled with all that Christ has attained and obtained. We have to exercise faith to such an extent that we can preach the gospel in a prevailing way. We must not pay attention to any feeling. Even if feelings do come, we have to tell the enemy, "I do not accept these feelings. I do not care what kind of feeling I have. As long as I have the will, the testament, in my hand, that is good enough. I believe in this will, and I believe in this work. I do not need any kind of manifestation, and I do not need any kind of feeling." Then we will see that the Holy Spirit honors us.

We must exercise the faith that anyone we touch will be saved. The evil one within us always causes us to doubt and ask how this can be. We must not try to figure it out by ourselves; rather, we have to exercise faith. If we do not believe that a person we touch can be saved, he will not be saved. The principle is that what is accomplished is according to our faith: "According to your faith, let it be done to you" (Matt. 9:29). We have to learn the lesson to exercise faith.

### BEING RIGHT WITH THE LORD, THE BODY, AND EVERY MEMBER OF THE BODY IN ORDER TO HAVE AUTHORITY, ASSURANCE, AND BOLDNESS

In order to exercise faith we have to be dealt with by the Lord. We have to be cleansed and have everything cleared up. If something within condemns us, we have to confess it and deal with it. If our conscience has some kind of accusation, our faith will be gone. We cannot take an indifferent attitude. We must take a positive attitude in faith, but this requires that we have everything cleared up and be cleansed. We have to confess and apply the blood for cleansing for whatever condemns us within. We should go to the Lord again and again to get ourselves cleansed and to make ourselves right with the Lord. Then we will have a pure conscience, a good conscience, a genuine conscience without any kind of offense. We can stand before the whole universe and tell the enemy, "Now my conscience is cleared up. I have no condemnation. I am void of any kind of offense, without accusation." If we are unable to work out certain matters, we should simply tell the Lord, "I am willing to do it, Lord, but I cannot. Cover me in this respect with Your precious blood." This will make us right with the Lord so that we will have boldness within.

Not only must we be right with the Lord, but when we go to preach the gospel, we have to get ourselves right with the Body and with all the members. If there is something between

us and the brothers, that will be a real hindrance, so we have
to deal with that hindrance and get right with the brothers. If
we are not right with the brothers, we will lose the ground.
The enemy, the devil, will laugh at us. This is the reality
in the spiritual world. The enemy knows whether or not we
are right with God, right with the Body, and right with the
members of the Body. We cannot fool him. If we are not right
in some matter with any member of the Body, then when we
go out to preach the gospel, the evil one will always hit this
weak point. We will not have the assurance, because there is
a weak point. Therefore, we have to get right with God, with
the Body, and with all the members. Then we can say, "I am
a person in this universe who is one hundred percent right
with God under the blood, and I am a member of the Body
of Christ who is one hundred percent right with all the
members. I have no problem with any member." Then we will
have assurance.

When we say that we have to pray much for the gospel
preaching, we mean that by praying we are dealt with by the
Lord very much. It is easy for sinners to be saved, but it is not
as easy for us to be dealt with thoroughly. We have to be dealt
with thoroughly by the Lord. Then we will be on the right
ground. Learn to exercise your faith, and learn to be dealt with
thoroughly. Then you will have the authority. I do not pay
much attention to the result of the preaching of the gospel,
but I pay my attention to the learning of the brothers. I am
still watching to see how much the brothers and sisters are
learning. This is the real building up. Some may say, "We are
still not built up, so we cannot go to preach." If this is so, then
you must be built up by being dealt with. We have to be dealt
with to get right with God, with the Body, and with every
member.

We have to learn the lessons. By the grace of the Lord, we
are now under the learning process. I have seen and I still am
seeing that all the brothers and the sisters are so willing to
learn the lessons. Do not pay attention to the result. Do not be
bothered by the numbers. We must be assured that a good
number of people will be brought in. There is no doubt about
that. The thing I am concerned for is that the brothers and

sisters would learn and be built up. I am concerned for how much we have learned, that is, how much we are being dealt with thoroughly by the Lord. To have this experience is wonderful. After the preaching of the gospel, we will see a glorious building up among us, plus some souls brought in among us; the result will be a positive gain. The main thing is the learning of the brothers and sisters. Before the preaching we may see weaknesses and problems, but after the preaching we wish to see that many dear brothers and sisters have been dealt with by the Lord. I believe that after we preach the gospel, many praises will go to the Lord, saying, "Lord, we thank You not only for the preaching, not only for the sinners being brought to Your Body, but for us, that we ourselves have learned so much, that we have been dealt with so much, that we have been built up so much, and that we have learned to know the spiritual world and all the devilish wiles."

In the future we will have more effectual preaching of the gospel. We will have the furtherance of the gospel, not only in this city but to other districts and even to other nations. After being trained in the military service, it is easy to be formed into an army. We also will learn the lessons and be trained; then it will be easy for us to be an army. If the Lord could have a prevailing expression of His church, the gospel will be very prevailing. It depends on the expression. Therefore, do not pay attention to the result, but pay attention to yourself.

## BEARING OUR RESPONSIBILITY
## TO HELP THE NEW CONVERTS TO GO ON

Do not think that it is good enough simply to bring people to be saved and to bring them to the church. Rather, that is only the delivery of the child. Mothers know that after a child is delivered, they will have many troubles. This is the main reason that mothers do not like to have many children; two or three are good enough. Nevertheless, in the church we need more deliveries, the more the better. We have to learn how to bear the responsibility, how to take care of the difficulties, and many other necessary matters. After the preaching of the gospel, we will be very busy. We are expecting many deliveries, so we see that we will have to take care of many things. For this reason, after our preaching of the gospel we should invite all the brothers and sisters and all those who hear the gospel to come together for follow-up meetings. Moreover, we hope on the following Lord's Day to have baptisms. As long as people are clear about their salvation, we have to baptize them right away. We have to learn how to take care of our responsibility. We have to learn much in this regard in order to help the new converts to go on. This is a tremendous responsibility, and many things are involved with it. Praise the Lord, these matters will afford us the best opportunity for us to learn and be trained in a practical way! May the Lord be merciful to us.

# CHAPTER THREE

# THE MEETING FOR PREACHING THE GOSPEL

Scripture Reading: Isa. 45:11

We have much to learn and practice concerning the preaching of the gospel. We will first consider the way to invite people to be saved. Some may say that this is very simple; it requires no training, and we know it already. Yes, we may know something about it, but there is a better technique for our practice.

## PRAYING WITH LIVING FAITH TO COMMAND THE LORD

First of all, we must trust in the Lord. We cannot do anything independently from the Lord. When we prepare to invite people, we must have adequate prayer about it. We need to pray to seek the Lord's mind concerning whom we contact. Then we must pray for the persons who we feel it is of the Lord that we invite them. We must remember them, bringing their names to the Lord day and night. We need to pray in a prevailing way. Isaiah 45:11 says, "Thus says Jehovah, / The Holy One of Israel and the One who formed him, / Ask Me about the things to come concerning My sons, / And concerning the work of My hands, command Me." In this verse the Lord gives us the ground to command Him. In a sense, He says, "I am your Servant. Give Me the order." We must learn to pray in this way, saying, "Lord, while I am here remaining with You and looking to You, I tell You that You have to do something."

There is the mysterious principle of faith in the universe. Faith honors the Lord, so the Lord always honors faith. To not have a living, prevailing, and powerful faith means that either we depend on ourselves or that we have an evil heart of unbelief. However, if we would not trust in and depend on ourselves, and if we believe, we will have the living faith to claim something, to command the Lord to do something. To command the Lord to do something means that we do not trust in ourselves and that we believe; the Lord will honor this faith. We need to pray in this way. All kinds of doubts come from the enemy. We must learn to believe and exercise a living faith.

Learn to pray for your contact with people, and learn to see how the Lord answers your prayer. Tell the Lord, "Lord, I need to see that You have saved at least one person I have prayed for." Tell this to Him definitely, challenging Him a little. Then you will see that He will come in. We can even say, "Lord, while I am praying here, at this very minute, You must work in the heart of the person for whom I am praying. I am waiting to hear a testimony from him that something happened within him at this very day, hour, and minute." Learn to prove the Lord, not as the people of Israel did in the wilderness with an evil heart of unbelief, but with a believing heart. If we have the living faith in prayer, we will have an impact in preaching. When we come to our friend, we will have the impact because we have prayed. Since we have commanded the Lord, we come to him with impact and assurance to tell him that he must be saved. This is the way to invite people. Luke 14:23 says that a master told his slaves not merely to invite but to compel people to come to his great dinner. Some versions translate *compel* as *force* or *constrain*. We have to compel, force, press, and constrain people to come.

## PRAYING WITH FASTING TO HAVE AN IMPACT

Before a meeting for preaching the gospel, we must find the way to contact the person or persons for whom we have been praying, either by phone or face to face, and on the day before the preaching, we should confirm that he is coming. Then on the morning of the preaching, we should fast. This is not something legal, but I believe it will please the Lord. If we mean business, we will not break our fast in the morning; we will keep our fast in order to pray. When Brother Watchman Nee was young and still in college, he fasted for all three meals on Saturday. He practiced this for over a year in order to pray, study the word, and remain with the Lord. Then on the Lord's Day he went to preach. His preaching was powerful with a real impact.

If we mean business with the Lord, He will mean business with us also, and we will have the impact. However, if we are indifferent with our preaching, the Lord will also be indifferent. The Lord can never work something out through lukewarm people; we must be cold or hot to the uttermost. We need to be "boiling" to the point that we "burn" people. How can we be boiling? It is by prayer and, if possible, though not in a legal way, by fasting. We should be burdened to fast and pray the morning of our preaching. We may pray, "Lord, the persons I have named before You so many times must be saved today. That is why I am here fasting. I have no interest in eating; I am already filled by this burden. I am full of Your work, so I have no interest and no capacity for eating." If we do this, we will see the impact and the answers to our prayers. If we pray and fast, then our day of preaching will be a day for crossing a boundary line. Before the day of Pentecost, the disciples prayed for ten days. They did not do anything in those ten days but pray. We can see the impact of their preaching.

After fasting and praying, before the meeting we should go to bring the persons we have prayed for. It is better to go to them; we should not trust them to come or merely believe their promise to come. Many times our friends give us a promise in a polite way, but after the meeting they apologize and give an excuse why they did not come. Rather, we should go to them to bring them and accompany them. Compel them to be saved. This is our regular duty and responsibility. From this time, if the Lord wills, we should do this every month until He comes. Every month we should preach the gospel.

Some say that it is too much to expect one hundred persons to be brought in. In the sense of unbelief, I agree with this. However, if we will all fast for one meal a day until the meeting for preaching the gospel, two hundred people may be saved. This depends not only on the Lord but very much on us and how we cooperate with the Lord. If we do not believe, and we all say, "Oh, that is impossible; let us forget about that and go to sleep," then not one person will be saved through us. This depends on how we cooperate with the Lord, with the church, and with one another.

## PREACHING BRINGING A REVIVAL TO THE CHURCH

If we have this practice in the preaching of the gospel, our life will be much improved. We will grow. For many years we may not have had much growth in life, but if we preach the gospel in this way, we will see the growth in life. Then the church will be increased both in quantity and in quality. The number of members is the quantity, and the growth of life is the quality. In the churches in the past, we learned the secret. For a long time many taught, preached, and built up, but there was no improvement. There was no result, and the brothers and sisters became tired of all those things. However, if we seek the Lord's mind, He will impress upon us that we have to do the work of preaching; we must burden the brothers and sisters with the preaching of the gospel. Simply by preaching the gospel, the church will be revived. By preaching, the church comes into life. It truly helps.

## FINISHING THE WORK WITH THE UNBELIEVERS IN ONE DAY

In order to do the work of inviting people in an effective way, we have to care for the matters above. We need to command the Lord, contact people, and pray and fast; then on the day of preaching we have to go to bring people, spending what we have to, even at a cost.

If possible, after the preaching we should also have lunch with the friend we invited. Many brothers and sisters were saved through this kind of lunch. During a preaching meeting the unbelievers are worked on, but sometimes the work is not finished. It is by having lunch with them that they will be saved. We need more time with them. We should not invite them the next day; we should do it right away after the meeting. When we start to cook something, we should finish cooking it. We should not allow it to remain raw and finish cooking it the next day. We will never finish in this way. We should do these things continuously in one day. If we say that the person for whom we are burdened should be saved on a definite day, the Lord will honor us. Do not be sloppy or indifferent; be diligent and compelling. In other things we have to be more patient to wait on the Lord, but in preaching we should not be as patient. We should tell the Lord, "Lord, I do not have the time to wait. You must do this for me quickly." Learn to do this, and try it. I am not speaking something I have not seen. Twenty years ago I did much preaching work, not only from the podium but also by invitations and visitations.

## STANDING WITH THE ONE WHO SPEAKS THE GOSPEL

If we do not have an adequate hall to meet in, the meeting for preaching may be crowded. We need to learn how to seat ourselves properly. We should give the seats to our friends, but we need at least one brother or sister to accompany two new ones. If there are one hundred unbelievers in the meeting, there should be fifty brothers and sisters with them. This makes a big difference. If the room is full of unbelievers, and all the brothers and sisters stand outside, leaving only one to give the message, the one who speaks will be stripped by the enemy. When a brother stands to speak, the other brothers should sit in the front or stand up with him. On the day of Pentecost, Peter stood up, and the eleven stood with him (Acts 2:14). When the brother says, "Friends, you have to believe in Jesus," the other brothers can say amen. This gives him weight; weight is added to the word. If a brother speaks and at least five or six stand with him, we will see the impact.

We have learned this lesson in casting out demons. The more brothers and sisters we have with us, the more impact we have. When I would go to cast out demons, I dared not do it by myself. I always brought as many brothers and sisters as possible to be with me. Then I was encouraged and strengthened, and I had the impact.

We need some brothers to accompany the speaker, and we also need many brothers and sisters to be present in the seats. Then there will be the impact. When a brother speaks, the brothers standing with him say amen, and the rest of the congregation also can say amen. This subdues the unbelievers, and it chases away the false, lying, and cheating spirit in their hearts. This can be compared to a ball game in which a team has more impact if more supporters attend the game.

## FIGHTING THE BATTLE
## BY OBSERVING THE UNBELIEVERS

We also need to learn to watch the unbelievers. If we see four unbelievers together, we have to make a readjustment by sitting with them to accompany them. In the process of the meeting, we can help them in prayer, singing, and the speaking. The preaching work is a real fight. We can help the speaking by cooperating with the speaker and by watching the unbelievers. There is a secret here. We may realize that a person is very inspired and moved by the Spirit. Then we can pray inwardly, "Lord, give him the secret to believing and being saved." If we pray like this, many times we will see that the person's face changes. At other times, we may realize that a person is stubborn, shaking his head in disagreement. Then we need to pray silently and inwardly, "Lord, bind the strong man, the rebellious one." By praying, we control the situation. This is the preaching of the church. Everyone is like the muscles of the body. Not only does the mouth speak, but every part of the body exercises. Then we will see the impact. In this way we should take our seat properly to help the preaching.

We need to exercise our whole being. First, of course, we exercise our spirit, and then we exercise our soul, our understanding, to watch people. If we learn to do this, we can even read their faces, and by their faces we can read their heart. There is no need to contact them after the meeting to know if they have been saved; we will know already. In this way, we need to help the unbelievers in prayer, in the hymns, and by watching them.

### CONTACTING PEOPLE AFTER THE MEETING

After the message, we have a short time to close the meeting by singing hymns or a chorus and by asking people to make a decision for the Lord. Then right away after that, the brothers and sisters have to contact two or three, or at least one person, to care for them. Before contacting them, we have watched them and noticed what kind of reaction they had. Based on this, we can contact them. This is a very important time; it is the time to reap the harvest, the time to deliver the child. In the travail of childbirth there is a certain time, the very point of time, at which to have the delivery. We all must learn to be the midwives. In the work after the gospel meeting, every one of us must be a good midwife, knowing how to deliver the child. Pray for this.

Concerning the work we do after the meeting, there are a few points to which we must pay our full attention. First, we should not talk too much, and we must not talk with vain words. Before we contact people, we will have watched them and noticed what kind of reaction they have had. Based on this, we can speak with them about the message. We must learn to talk in a brief way to "close the deal," just like a salesman. If we talk too much, there will be no deal. Our purpose is not to talk. Some brothers use the time after the meeting just to talk about everything, from Genesis to Revelation, from the moon to the sun, and from the ancestors to the modern generation. They have much to say, but eventually they do not make the deal.

We need to close the deal in a brief way by helping people to pray. After we speak with someone for two or three minutes, five or six at the most, we have to influence them to pray. We must learn the secret of how to help people to pray. Many times people will say that they do not know how to pray, so we can ask them to follow us in prayer. We can say, "I will pray something, then you follow me; say the same thing from your heart." In a simple way we have to help people to confess their sins, recognize that the Lord Jesus is the Son of God, the very Savior and Redeemer, and receive and accept the Lord Jesus personally as their Savior. We should also help them to realize that by Christ's redeeming death, by the cross of Christ, their sins have been forgiven. We need to pray with them in a very brief, effective, and definite way. The Lord honors this kind of prayer. After this kind of prayer, many persons have had a change in their life, and the Holy Spirit becomes real and living to them. By this kind of prayer, the Holy Spirit truly touches the hearts and spirits of people.

After the prayer, it is very good to give people one or two verses from the Scriptures according to their situation, the verses which are best suited to each case respectively. For some people John 3:16 is good, and for others Romans 6:23 is good. We should give one or two verses as a confirmation and help them to grasp or be grasped by the verses. A living word from the Bible is a confirmation to a new believer, a proof of their salvation in a brief way.

After the prayer, we should also have a friendly talk with the person. Ask him how and with whom he came, and take down his name and address. However, we should do this in a flexible, spontaneous way, not in a legal way. If the person he came with has his name and address already, there is no need for you to get it.

## BAPTIZING THE NEW BELIEVERS

Before the meeting for preaching, we should have another time for visitation. Then the brothers and sisters can turn in dated sheets of paper with the name and address of their friends and some remarks about them, such as whether or not they have been saved. Then by those sheets we will know how many have been influenced by our preaching and what we must do in the meeting. If ten or twenty have already been saved, then on the next Lord's Day we should have a baptism for them. Do not think this is too fast; there is no need to wait. The Scriptures say that people should be baptized as soon as they believe (Mark 16:16; Acts 2:38, 41; 8:36-38; 22:16). Believing is only half a step; believing and being baptized are the whole step of being saved. We do not believe in water baptism in a superstitious way, as some do. However, we do believe that there is something particular in baptism. In the past I saw sick people who were healed after their baptism, and some experienced the outpouring of the Holy Spirit. There are many cases like this. Baptism is not a form or a superstition; rather, we believe it is necessary because the Lord commanded it. After the preaching we should have a baptism, the earlier the better.

There may be a number of new ones who are not clear about salvation and baptism, so we must follow up with them within a few weeks. Then when they are clear, we will have another baptism. There will be many things to do until we bring all these people into the church life, and the brothers and sisters can care for them as new members. Our work must be completed by their being brought into the church life; otherwise, we must care for them some more. If one of our friends is not saved in the preaching, then we have to care for him in a second meeting for preaching in the following month.

# Chapter Four

# A GOSPEL MESSAGE

Scripture Reading: Eph. 2:11-12

Ephesians 2:11 and 12 say, "Therefore remember that once you, the Gentiles in the flesh, those who are called uncircumcision by that which is called circumcision in the flesh made by hands, that you were at that time apart from Christ, alienated from the commonwealth of Israel, and strangers to the covenants of the promise, having no hope and without God in the world." I would like to impress you with these three short phrases: *apart from Christ, having no hope,* and *without God.* When a man is apart from Christ, he has no hope. Do you have Christ? Is Christ within you? Those who are apart from Christ, who have no hope, and who are without God are pitiful.

## THE MYSTERY OF HUMAN LIFE

Still, we humans are the most wonderful creatures on this earth. We have a mind to think, emotions to love, and a heart to desire things. Moreover, we have even something deeper than the heart, that is, our inmost part, the human spirit, to seek something better, higher, and more important. That something is the very God. Many times when I was alone, I considered a little about man and said, "How wonderful he is! He can do many things. He can study. He can invent. He can even get a doctoral degree." However, I would ask you, what is the real meaning of human life? What is the real meaning of the life of such wonderful persons that you are? Why are you existing on this earth? Is it only for clothing, eating, and sleeping? In past generations, in century after century, many thoughtful people, philosophers, and wise and learned men did their best to find the answer. We can find many books in the libraries written by these wise men, telling us this and that. However, none of those answers is satisfactory, because they all neglect the source of man.

What is the source of man? God the Creator is the source. Man was created by God. In order to know the purpose of something, we need to go the manufacturer, the maker, and ask him why he made it. If we did not know what a soft drink bottle is, we may consider it to be strange yet meaningful. We would ask for what purpose it was made. Someone may say, "I do not know. Maybe it is to hit people with, or maybe it is for children to play with." I would respond, "Sir, you had better go to the maker and ask him for what purpose he manufactured this strange thing. To be sure, he will tell you that he purposely made it as a vessel to contain something."

## MAN CREATED AS A VESSEL TO CONTAIN GOD

Romans 9 tells us that we human beings are vessels made by God. God is the Potter, and we are the clay, and out of clay God made us as vessels. We know that a vessel is a container to contain something. A bottle is a vessel, and a cup is also a vessel, a container. Even a lightbulb is a vessel to contain electricity. If the purpose of a lightbulb was not to contain electricity, it would indeed be a strange thing. It looks like a ball, but it is not good to play with. What would be the use of it? It would be useless, just a waste. Today, however, we know that a lightbulb is not only useful but important. It contains electricity, expresses the light of electricity, and brings all of us into the light.

We too were made by God as vessels, containers, but what were we made to contain? This is a real problem. A soft drink bottle is a vessel to contain soft drink, a cup is a container for juice at breakfast time, and a lightbulb is a container to contain electricity. As containers made by God, are we made to contain and absorb knowledge? No, because we know that knowledge does not satisfy. The more knowledge you gain, the more emptiness you sense. Then what were we made to contain, receive, and absorb? It is hard for many people to say.

Friends, there is no need for me to argue with you, and

there is no need for me to prove to you that in this universe, even today so close to you, so near to you, is God Himself. Today He is Christ, He is the Savior, the Lord Jesus. He is the very God. He is like the air, and He is like radio waves. He is everywhere, omnipresent, and He is waiting for you. You were made purposely as a vessel to contain Him.

### OUR SPIRITUAL THIRST AND HUNGER BEING SATISFIED ONLY BY GOD IN CHRIST

I can illustrate this in the following way. Look at ourselves. We have ears, eyes, a nose, and a mouth. Within we have a mind and a stomach. With our mouth we take in water and food, and then we store the water and food in our stomach. With our ears we receive music, voices, and songs. With our eyes we apprehend the colorful scenery, and with our nose we take in the sweet odor. Suppose that you are thirsty, but there was no water. What shall you do? You can do nothing but die. Suppose that you are hungry within, but there was no food supply on the whole earth. What could you do? Again, you could do nothing but die. Do you realize that today you have a spiritual thirst and a spiritual hunger within you? This thirst and this hunger can never be quenched or satisfied by anything other than God Himself in Christ.

Regardless of how much wealth you gain, what kind of degree you obtain, and what kind of position or rank you attain, if you do not have Christ within, there is a real thirst and a real hunger within you. Praise the Lord, He created us in such a way! He created a spirit within us so that we may contact Him and receive Him. You have such an organ. In a little radio there is a receiver; it is a receiving "organ." Why did someone make this receiver? It was made purposely to receive radio waves. Why is there a part—very deep within your being—that is always thirsty and hungry? Why is it that the richer you get, the more hunger you have within? It is because there is a receiving organ within you created purposely by God. That is the human spirit. God is spirit, and those who worship Him must worship Him in spirit, in the human spirit. You have a spirit within you. Day by day that is your problem. If you did not have a spirit, you would not have this deeper thirst and hunger. It is because God created a spirit within you as a receiving organ so that you are always hungry and thirsty for something deeper and something higher. That something deeper and higher is God Himself in Christ.

## BEING FILLED WITH CHRIST
## TO SATISFY OUR EMPTINESS

In 1937 when I was preaching the gospel in Nanking, China, a smart, modern, highly cultured young lady came to me and said, "Mr. Lee, I like what you have preached. I appreciate it, and I would like to believe, but I am afraid of one thing. From my youth I have gone to the opera to see the dramas. This is my habit and a part of my makeup. I am afraid that after I receive Christ, I will have no more liberty to go to the opera. I want Christ, yet I do not want to give up the opera. Please tell me, after I become a Christian, can I still go to the opera?" To answer that question was a real problem. I realized that if I answered no, then she would not become a Christian, but if I said that it does not matter, she would be wrongly encouraged. She had her son with her, a boy about four years old. I said, "Suppose this little boy had a sharp knife in his hand. That is very dangerous. What would you do to get rid of the knife?" She said it would be easy. She would simply throw some candy on the floor, and the boy would take it. Then if she put some delicious fruit down, the boy would drop the knife and pick up the fruit. I said, "You are right. Why would this boy want to take the knife? It is because his hands are empty. Why do you like the opera so much? It is because you are empty. One day when you are filled with Christ, with the better 'candy,' you will drop what is not as good. There is no need for me to tell you whether or not you still can go to the opera. If you receive Christ, you will know. You are empty, so you are desirous of many things to fill up the void. However, nothing can fill up the void within you but Christ. You have to receive Christ. Christ is the only One who can fill." At this point the woman was saved.

Friends, you have heard that God is gracious. Moreover, Christ is omnipresent. He is even at your mouth waiting for you to call Him "Lord Jesus." He is waiting at the door of your heart for you to receive Him. Oh, just open your heart and tell Him, "Lord Jesus, I need You. This morning I make a decision to receive You."

## USING OUR HUMAN SPIRIT
### AS THE PROPER ORGAN TO RECEIVE GOD

Here is a little secret. Twenty-six years ago I was preaching the gospel at a college. After four days of preaching, a very learned man, who was a judge in the local court, came to me and said, "I am very interested in what you have been preaching, but I do not know how to get it." I said, "Sir, to contact or receive anything you have to use the right organ. If you are going to receive music, you have to exercise your ears. If you are going to take in the beautiful scenery, you have to exercise your eyes. Suppose there is a sweet odor here. If you do not exercise your nose, but merely use your eyes to look at the odor, where would the odor be? You may say, 'You are lying. There is no odor because I cannot see it.' The reason you cannot substantiate the odor is that you are using the wrong organ. If you use your nose, then right away you will substantiate the very substance of the odor. In order to substantiate any substance, you have to exercise the right organ. God is a Spirit. You cannot substantiate Him by your thinking or by your looking around. You have to substantiate Him by your spirit. Forget about your thinking. Close your eyes, and open your heart and your spirit. Simply say, 'Lord Jesus, my God, my Savior!' Right away you will sense the reality of Christ within you. You will substantiate the reality, the substance of Christ, within you."

Friends, there is no need for us to say any more. Now is the time for you to make the decision for Christ, to open yourselves to receive Christ as the reality. He is the living and omnipresent Spirit, and you have a spirit, not only a body and a mind, not only a soul, but a spirit deep within you. Forget about your body, forget about where you are, and forget about your mind and emotion. Simply open yourselves from your inmost part to this Christ who is waiting at your heart and at your mouth. Simply open to Him and say, "Lord Jesus,

I accept You this morning." You will contact Him, and He will contact you. Please make such a vital decision for Christ at this time. It is a glory to make a decision for Christ. Do not hesitate, and do not lose this opportunity. He is waiting, and He is knocking at your heart. Receive Him, and receive Him now.

# CHAPTER FIVE

# THE PERSON AND WORK OF CHRIST FOR OUR SALVATION

Scripture Reading: John 1:1, 14, 18; Isa. 9:6; 1 Pet. 2:24; Isa. 53:6; 1 John 5:12; Acts 10:43

Not all those who hear the preaching of the gospel make the decision publicly to receive the Lord, but they still may have a heart for the Lord. Through their further contact with the saints, we may learn that they indeed have been saved. We all have to learn how to help these new ones to realize the Lord's salvation in a full way. On the one hand, the new believers must be clear about the Lord's salvation, and on the other hand, we need to know how to work with these new believers to help them to know this salvation. When a person receives Jesus Christ the Lord as the Savior, there are two categories of things we must take care of. The first is that there are many things we must know as believers of the Lord Jesus, and the second category is that there are many things to practice. After we receive Christ as our Savior, right away we have to know many matters and practice many items. Many dear brothers and sisters, even among us, are not clear about the main items that Christians must know and practice. In this message we will see the things that we have to know.

## THE PERSON OF CHRIST

### The Word, Who Is God Expressed

The first matter that we must be clear about is the person of Christ. We have to know the person of Christ, that is, who Christ is. This is a great matter in human history. For two thousand years many historians have studied and discussed this matter: Who is Jesus Christ; what is the person of Christ? In a simple way I would recommend you to the Bible. Please open the Bible and read the Gospel of John. John 1:1 says, "In the beginning was the Word, and the Word was with God, and the Word was God." The Word is Christ, and this Word which is Christ was with God, and this Word which is Christ was even God Himself. Then verse 14 says, "And the Word became flesh and tabernacled among us (and we beheld His glory, glory as of the only Begotten from the Father), full of grace and reality." At least three titles are given here to this one person, who is Christ. He is the Word, this Word is God, and verse 14 tells us that He is the only begotten Son of the Father. This is very meaningful, even very strange, to our thought. On the one hand, this Christ is God Himself; on the other hand, this Christ is the only begotten Son of God. Verse 18 says, "No one has ever seen God; the only begotten Son, who is in the bosom of the Father, He has declared Him." I wish to ask you to consider these verses, because the mystery of the person of Christ is in them.

In these few verses we are first told that Christ is the Word of God. It is easy for us to understand what the Word is. A word is an expression. My word is my expression; if I stand here and shut my mouth, not speaking a word, you cannot understand what I have within me. What I have within me will be a mystery, because it can be expressed only in my word. Christ is the Word of God; this means that Christ is the expression of God. God Himself is the reality, yet He is hidden and mysterious. Christ is the Word of God, so He is the explanation and definition of God. Christ is God expressed.

## God Himself

Second, these verses show us that the Word is God Himself. This means that Christ is God Himself. Many people, even Christians, often have a wrong thought, supposing that Christ is a separate person from God. This is wrong. Do not think that Christ is a separate person from God—that God is God, Christ is Christ, and these are two separate persons. We have to realize that God is in Christ, and Christ is one with God. This is why verse 18 says that no man has ever seen God, but the only begotten Son of God has declared Him. God is in Christ, and Christ is the very embodiment of God, the very expression of God. In a simple word to new believers, I would say that we all have to recognize that Christ is the very God.

## Incarnated with the Human Nature

In these few verses there is another point. This very Christ who is the Word of God and who is God Himself, the very expression and embodiment of God, the only begotten Son of God, one day about two thousand years ago was made flesh; He was incarnated. Before two thousand years ago, He was God only, but at the time of His incarnation, the time when He was born as a man, He took the human nature upon Himself. Christ was incarnated; He came to be a man. Now by this incarnation there is something more with Him. Many times I illustrate this in the following way. I may have a handkerchief made of white cotton and nothing else, but one day I dip this handkerchief into a green dye. The handkerchief then becomes cotton mingled with dye. It is no more only white; it has become green. However, the substance is still there. There is no change of substance; only the form, the appearance, has changed. Now two things mingle together as one. Two thousand years ago before the incarnation, Christ was God only. He was the very Creator of the whole universe. But one day He came into the flesh of man. He "dipped" Himself into human nature. He was dyed in the human color, and He was named with a human name, the name of Jesus. The "handkerchief" became green, but within this green cloth is the reality, the substance, of the handkerchief. Within this little man Jesus is God. God became "colored" with man, with human nature.

Isaiah 9:6 says, "For a child is born to us, / A son is given to us; / And the government / Is upon His shoulder; / And His name will be called / Wonderful Counselor, / Mighty God, / Eternal Father, / Prince of Peace." We know that this happened in a manger in Bethlehem. In Bethlehem, one day in a manger a child was born and a son was given. The child born to us is called Mighty God. He was truly a child, but within Him is the mighty God. He was really a "green cloth," but within is the substance of the "handkerchief." We can say that the handkerchief is something green, but we have to realize that it is still a handkerchief. A little child, even a babe born in the manger, is called Mighty God because He is God incarnated. He is God made to be flesh.

We all have to realize that the very Christ in whom we believe is the very God Himself. He is the Creator, the only God, the unique God in this universe. One day He became a man, being incarnated to dwell with man. His appearance was absolutely in the form of a man, but within Him was God Himself. Christ is God in man. Within this man is God; He can never be separated from God, and God can never be separated from Him. Without Him, we do not have God. God is in Christ, and strictly speaking Christ is God.

## Crucified and Resurrected

One day He went to the cross. He was crucified and He died there. However, because He is the very God, the source of life, after He died, He resurrected. It may seem rather difficult to believe in the resurrection of Christ. In the Bible, however, we have a very good illustration, that of a grain of wheat. When someone sows a seed, he buries the seed in the soil, and the seed dies. It truly dies, but after death something grows up. In 1936 I went to the old capital of China, Beijing, and I was invited to the home of a professor at one of the biggest universities in China, to help some young students to believe in the Lord Jesus. After my preaching, an intelligent young student came to me and said, "Mr. Lee, there is one thing that I cannot get through. If you can help me to get through it, then I will believe what you are preaching here. I cannot believe that a person can die and then be resurrected." On that campus there were some fields of wheat growing in the wintertime in North China. I pointed through the window and said, "Look at those grains of wheat. Do you see resurrection there? Just two months ago people sowed the seeds into the earth. The seeds died there, but after death something grew up. The seeds resurrected because within the seeds there is a powerful, dynamic life. You can bury a seed, but you cannot bury the life in it. If you bury a piece of rock, it is really buried, and that is the end. Nothing will grow up because there is no life. If you bury a seed, however, after a certain amount of time it grows up. Christ is the very God who is the source of life. To put Him into death was not to put Him to an end; that simply helped Him to grow up. Within Him there is life, and this life is a very dynamic power to grow in Him. Christ died on the cross, and then He resurrected.

"A seed has a certain kind of form, but after it dies and grows up, the form changes. After His resurrection, Christ changed in form; He was transformed. This is something too wonderful and too mysterious, beyond our understanding. Can you explain how a small round seed after death and resurrection becomes tall and green? Only God understands the law, the principle, which governs a seed. One little round seed grows up to be a tree, another grows up to be a flower, and another grows up to be wheat. Moreover, all wheat is of the same form. There must be a law governing that, which only God knows." Through this illustration, that young man in the university was saved that day. After he believed, he started to love the Lord, and he was very much used by the Lord. Today he is a leading one in the church in his locality.

I wish to impress you that Christ is the most wonderful One in this universe. He is God, and He is the very Creator. One day He became a man; then He died on the cross, He resurrected, and He has been transformed into a wonderful form. Today He is firstly called the Savior and then the Lord. Moreover, He is also the Spirit. If I had the time, I would refer you to all the verses that tell us these things. When Christ was crucified on the cross, He was the Redeemer. Now today, after His resurrection, He is the Spirit as the living Savior. He is the mighty Savior, the Lord, and the Spirit. He is the Spirit; this means that He is just like the air, so available to us. Wherever we are, there He is, and wherever we go, there He goes, just like the air. We cannot separate ourselves from the air. Today we have the word *pneumatic*. This is what the Spirit is. Christ is the very Spirit today. I repeat: He is God, the Creator; one day He became a man, and he died on the cross as the Redeemer to redeem us; then He resurrected and was transformed into the Spirit. Now today He is the Spirit as the living Savior, and He is our Lord. As the Spirit, He is everywhere; He is so available. When we receive Him, we receive Him as an all-inclusive One. In Him is God. In Him is the Creator. In Him is man, the Redeemer, and the Savior. In Him we have the Lord, and He is the very Spirit. This is the first item we have to know. I am presenting these items to you in a very brief and simple way.

## THE WORK OF CHRIST IN HIS DEATH

We must also know the purpose for Christ's death on the cross. First Peter 2:24 says, "Who Himself bore up our sins in His body on the tree, in order that we, having died to sins, might live to righteousness; by whose bruise you were healed." *The tree* refers to the cross. For what purpose did Christ die on the cross? It says here clearly that Christ died on the cross to bear our sins. In the Old Testament, Isaiah 53:6 says, "We all like sheep have gone astray; / Each of us has turned to his own way, / And Jehovah has caused the iniquity of us all / To fall on Him." When Christ died on the cross, God laid all our sins, all our iniquities, on Him. Here, therefore, is the forgiveness of sins and the remission of sins for us. We all have to realize that Christ died on the cross to bear our sins. This is what we call the work of Christ. We do have the problem of our sins, but praise Him, He died on the cross and took away all our sins! Our problem of sins was solved on the cross.

## THE SALVATION PREPARED BY CHRIST FOR US

As we have seen, Christ is God, He became a man, as our Redeemer He was crucified on the cross to take away all our sins, and He resurrected to be our Savior, our Lord as the Spirit. Now because Christ is such a person and because He has died in such a way, salvation is ready for you. Within this salvation there are several things which are very important for you. First, in this salvation you have forgiveness of sins. Acts 10:43 says, "To this One all the prophets testify that through His name everyone who believes into Him will receive forgiveness of sins." When you believe in this Christ and receive Him as your Savior, forgiveness of sins becomes your portion. You share in and partake of this portion. Forgiveness of sins is in the salvation prepared by Christ for you.

Within this salvation, you also have the eternal life, the divine life. First John 5:12 says, "He who has the Son has the life; he who does not have the Son of God does not have the life." If you believe in Christ, you have Christ, and when you have Christ, you have the life. Many verses tell us the same things, but the above two verses are adequate. They tell us that the remission and forgiveness of sins is in the salvation prepared for you by Christ, and within this salvation you have the divine, eternal life of God. These are the two main items of the salvation of God, the salvation prepared for you by Christ.

## THE WAY TO RECEIVE AND ENJOY SALVATION

### Recognizing Christ's Person and Work

We have seen the person of Christ, the work of Christ, and the salvation prepared for us by Christ. Now, what is the proper way to receive and enjoy this salvation? You have to do three things. First, you have to recognize that this Christ is the very God, the Creator, and that He became a man, died on the cross for your sins, and resurrected from the dead. Now He is the living Savior, the Lord as the Spirit. He is living, real, and available to you. Tell Christ that you do recognize Him as such. Tell him, "Lord, I recognize that You are the very God. One day You became a man, and You died for me on the cross. You have taken away all my sins. Then You resurrected from the dead. Today I do recognize that You are the living Savior. You are my Savior, and You are my Lord. Now You are the Spirit, who is so available to me. You are now with me and even within me."

When I was saved forty years ago, I did not receive the help that we are fellowshipping about here. It took me more than ten years to realize all these things. However, today there is no need for you to take ten years. Just one night is good enough, perhaps even one hour. This is a very brief statement of the whole gospel from the Scriptures. You need to recognize these truths. This kind of recognition is very necessary.

## Contacting Christ with Our Human Spirit by Speaking to Him

Second, you have to contact Him. To recognize is something in your mentality, your understanding, but to contact Him is something different. As we have pointed out, to contact anything you have to exercise the right organ. To contact my voice, for example, you must exercise your ears. Now Christ is the Spirit, so you have to exercise your human spirit to contact Him. The spirit is the deepest, inmost part of your whole being. To contact Christ, realizing that He is the living Savior and the Spirit, you simply must exercise the inmost part of your being to talk with Him. Many times I have told people not to compose a prayer. Simply be like a little child who comes to his mother. When a little child comes to his mother, there is no need for him to compose anything. He simply expresses what he feels within. Simply come to Christ; realize that He is so living and that He is the Spirit so available and close to you. Then express yourself from the very inmost part of your being. Whatever you feel within, just tell Him, even with broken sentences. If you feel that you are wrong with God or wrong with man—whether with your parents, with your schoolmate, or with others—simply tell Him, "Lord Jesus, I am wrong. I am wrong with God. I am wrong with certain persons. I am wrong with so many things." Just tell Him. Do not consider how to compose your utterance. There is no need for that. Simply express yourself from within. If you feel that you are sorrowful and have much trouble, just tell Him, "Lord, I am so sorrowful. I have so many problems." Tell Him what your problems are in a living, practical way.

In the previous message I recounted how I preached the gospel to a judge. He asked me how he could believe, and I told him that he had to exercise the right organ. If you exercise your nose to smell a voice, you cannot substantiate it. If you exercise your eyes to look at the voice, you cannot receive it. However, if you exercise your ears, the hearing organ will

substantiate the substance of the voice. The right organ to substantiate Christ is your human spirit, your inmost part. That
day I also told the judge, "Sir, I suggest you go home tonight,
close your door, and talk with Christ." He asked me in what
way he should talk. I said, "In whatever way you can. Simply
talk." He did this. He went back that night and told his wife
and his only child, "Please go to the other room. I have some
business to do." He closed the door and knelt down. His wife
looked into the room through the window. What a surprise
that was. She said, "What is he doing there? This is something completely new." He prayed there, and then he went to
sleep. Nothing seemed to happen at that time. Later, however, he told me that the next morning, while he was going to
court to take care of a case, the whole universe changed. The
heavens, the earth, and everything was new. Everything was
lovely. He looked at a dog, and the dog was lovely. He looked
at a cat, and the cat was lovely. He looked at everything, and
everything was lovely. He began to laugh. While he was
taking care of his case, he was laughing in the court. The sec-
retary and the other people could not understand what had
happened to this judge.

At noontime he went back home, rejoicing and laughing all
the way. When he got home, his wife asked him, "What? Did
you find a million dollars? What makes you so happy?" He
said, "I do not know; I am just happy." Then he referred himself to one of the young brothers who was a student in college.
That young brother told him, "Sir, you have to realize that
this is salvation. You have already shared in salvation." Not
long after that, the judge gave up his position. As an elderly
brother in Taiwan, he recently went to the Lord.

Try this, dear friends. I would suggest that tonight you
find a place to be in private with Christ. Open yourself from
your inmost part to say something to Him. You do not need to
compose anything. Simply tell Him what you have on your
heart. Tell him in broken language. Tell him in such a way as
to contact Him. Do not do this only once for all. This is just a
start. From this time on, time after time you have to contact
Christ. If you would ask me how many times I contact Christ
daily, I could not tell you. All the time I simply contact this

living Christ. I do not even have a definite time for this kind of prayer. I pray all the time. He is just as the air to me; I simply live in this way. Can you tell me how many times you breathe every day? If you can, I am afraid that you are seriously sick, struggling to breathe once, twice, and a third time. If you are a healthy person, though, you do not know how many times you breathe. All the time you just breathe. You need to contact Christ your Savior in such a living way. Forget about Christianity; forget about religion. We are not helping you to receive a religion. We are helping you to realize such a living One, the living Christ. Learn to recognize Him and contact Him.

We all need to learn how to receive Christ. This means that you have to open yourself from within. You have to open your whole being to Christ and tell Him, "Lord Jesus, not only do I recognize You as my Savior, but now I open myself to You and receive You into me as my life and my everything." Not many Christians know how to do this, and not many practice to do this. To pray is one thing, but to receive Christ is another. Many persons pray to Christ, but they do not have the realization of how much they have to receive Christ. We have to learn that we must receive Christ. He is living and real, so you must open yourself to receive Him again and again. We all have to learn to receive the living Christ, not merely a religion.

Regrettably, today millions of people are Christians in name. They have taken the religion, but they have not received Christ Himself. I have been to Europe a few times. In France or Belgium, if you ask people, "Are you a Christian?" they may say, "Why not?" I learned not to ask people in this way. If you ask this, you will offend them. One day in the Philippines when I took a taxi, I had the thought to ask the driver if he was a Christian. He also was offended. He said, "Why not? If I am not a Christian, then what am I?" However, this is a Christian only in name, a Christian in religion. I realized that he did not have Christ within him. To have Christianity is one thing, but to have Christ is another. In actuality, there is not such a word as *Christianity* in the Scriptures. Rather, there is Christ. What we are doing is not to help you to accept Christianity as a religion. We are helping you to realize the proper way to receive the living Christ into you. What you need is not Christianity but Christ Himself.

Some may ask how they can receive Christ. The way to receive Christ is to open yourself to Him. Simply open to Him all the time. He is the Spirit, and He is now within you. Learn to open yourself to Him all the time, saying, "Lord Jesus, I am closed to everything else but open to You." I can assure you that whether tonight or tomorrow, or this week or next week, something will happen to you within. You will receive the reality. You will sense the loveliness of Christ, and you will sense the light, the power, the life, and the love of Christ within you.

You must recognize Christ as the One we have spoken of here, and you have to contact Him. Always say something to Him, not from your mentality but from your heart and spirit, from your inmost part. You should not hate anyone, but even if you do hate someone, you should tell Christ, "Lord Jesus, now I am going to hate someone. Lord, be with me while I hate him." Simply say a word to Him. Then He will help you to know how to hate. He will help you to know whether or not to hate that person, and eventually He will help you to drop your hating. Simply speak to Him. Make him a Friend in whatever you do. If you are going to a movie, just tell Him, "Lord Jesus, I am interested in the movie, and I am going to see it." Talk with Him. This is the best way for you to contact Christ.

Learn to say something to Christ. Do not keep anything hidden from Him. Be exposed and open before Christ. Tell Him everything that is on your heart, open to Him, and learn always to receive Him. This is the best prayer.

## TAKING THE WORD OF THE SCRIPTURES
## FOR THE ASSURANCE OF SALVATION

You also need to be confirmed by the word of the Scriptures. In other words, you have to take the word of the Scriptures for the assurance of salvation. If you recognize the person of Christ and that Christ died to bear your sins, and if you receive His salvation and pray and open yourself to receive Him, then you need to know according to the word of the Bible that you are saved. The Bible has many verses that say you are saved. Your sins are forgiven, Christ today is within you, and you have the eternal life; therefore, you are saved. In the Scriptures there are many verses of such an assurance and confirmation of salvation. Now, by this assurance and confirmation, you have to be at peace that you are saved. You are a person saved by Christ, and you are a son of God, a child of God. This is wonderful! Do not look to anything else. Gradually, day by day from now on, this living Lord will work out many things with you and within you.

I would ask you to realize the above five points: who Christ is, what Christ did for you, the salvation prepared for you, the proper way to partake of this salvation, and the full assurance of this salvation in the Bible. Recognize that the Christ in whom you believe is the very God, that He became a man and died on the cross for your sins, and that He resurrected. Today He is the Spirit as the living Savior and the almighty Lord. Recognize this, open yourself to Him, and contact Him in a living way. I assure you then that you are saved. This is not confirmed by me but by this covenant, this testament, this will. It is confirmed, so you have the assurance of salvation. So you have to say, "Hallelujah, praise the Lord! I am saved. Regardless of how evil and how pitiful I am, I am saved!" Then whenever you sense you are wrong, simply confess. It is very easy, and it is so pleasant. To confess to Him whatever you sense within is a pleasant way to contact Christ.

## WORKING WITH PEOPLE IN LOVE AND IN PATIENCE

All the new ones can be helped by this message, but this speaking is also for all the brothers and sisters. You will have more time to contact people and work with the promising ones in this way. Help them to realize these five points, and work these five points into them. Maybe you cannot work out all these points in one night. I have done it in a brief way, but please do not be as brief with them. You need some time to deal just with the first item. Help them to open the Bible, read it, and understand it word by word. Then after three or four contacts like this, they will be helped to be very clear. The Holy Spirit always follows this kind of work. We simply pave the way. The more we work in this way, the more the Holy Spirit will follow, and He will work it out. People will be impressed, painted, and anointed by the Holy Spirit. Then you will see the difference. We have to learn to work with people in love and in patience. I believe that in these days people will be helped not only to be saved but also to be very clear about the way of salvation.

CHAPTER SIX

## BASIC PRACTICES FOR OUR SALVATION

Scripture Reading: Acts 20:21; 1 John 1:9; 3:4; 5:17a; Rom. 10:9; Acts 2:38

In the previous message we saw that in order to receive Christ as the Savior, a person must first realize who Christ is; that is, he has to know the person of Christ. Second, he needs to know the work of Christ, what Christ has done for him and for what purpose Christ died on the cross. The death of the cross is the work of Christ. Then he must know the salvation prepared by Christ. Within this salvation, there are the remission of sins and the imparting of the divine life. In order to receive Christ as the Savior, a person also has to contact Him. We are not dealing with a religion. We are not dealing with doctrines or learning teachings. Rather, we are dealing with the living One who is just like the air. We have to breathe Him in. We have to contact Him. Fifth, in order to contact and receive Him, we have to open ourselves to the Lord, not merely outwardly but inwardly, from the deepest part of our whole being. We may compare this to opening a window to the fresh air. If we close the window, we close off the fresh air. In order to receive fresh air into a room, we have to open the window widely and thoroughly. Christ is the Spirit, just like the fresh air. If we are going to enjoy Him and receive Him into us, we must open ourselves, the more the better and the deeper the better. We have to realize and be clear about these five items.

There are also five things that a person must practice in the process of receiving Christ as the Savior. To receive Christ is mainly to believe in Him, but this believing includes several matters, so we may say that there is a process of believing. A process is one thing that includes several steps, or several points. Many Christians are short of some of these five items. They may not be short of all five, but they may be short of one or two of them.

## A THOROUGH REPENTANCE TO GOD

The first thing we must practice is a thorough repentance to God. Repentance is the first step of our real believing, our prevailing faith in Christ. If we do not have a real repentance, that means our believing is not so real. In order to have a real believing, a true faith in Christ, we must have a real and thorough repentance. The order in the Scriptures is *repent* and *believe*. Repentance must go ahead of faith. Acts 20:21 says, "Solemnly testifying both to Jews and to Greeks repentance unto God and faith in our Lord Jesus." Repentance is unto God, and faith is in the Lord Jesus. Repentance unto God and living faith in the Lord Jesus are the testimony of the apostle Paul.

The Greek word for *repent* means a change of mind, or a turn of mind. Repentance is a turning. We have to turn, because we are away from God, and we have gone astray from God. God is in one direction, but our whole life and living are in another direction. We are not toward God but against God. Our whole living first includes our thinking, our mind. Our way of thinking is not toward God; it is away from God. This is also true of our behavior, our conduct, and our family life. It is even true of our schooling, our business, and our friendships. Even our clothing and our driving are not toward God but against God, away from God. In almost everything of our human life we are away from God; we are not toward God but against God.

The gospel of God demands that we repent, that is, that we have a turn. This is not only a left turn or right turn, but it is a U-turn. We have to turn back to God. We must point not our back but our face toward God. God is in one direction, but we are living and walking in another. Everything related to us is toward the wrong direction, so the more we live, the more we are away from God and the further we go astray from God.

Now God demands that we repent. This means that we have to turn back toward God. This is repentance toward God.

Everything related to us has to be turned: our study, schooling, marriage, family life, relationships with friends, relationships with relatives, spending of money, clothing, thinking, decisions, motives, intents, and every other thing. Everything related to us within and without must be turned to God. This is the real meaning of repentance. We must have a thorough change in our life, a U-turn in our whole life. In the preaching of the gospel, we all have to learn the lesson to help people take this kind of U-turn.

How much we repent depends on how much we have turned. Some Christians indeed have a certain kind of repentance, but they turn only a little; they have only a little change. A brother may have some change, but to what degree? Has he turned 45 degrees, 90 degrees, or 180 degrees? Some turn a full 360 degrees, turning around to be the same as before. We need a 180 degree turn, a real U-turn back to God. How much we are able to help others depends on how much we have turned, that is, how much we have repented. We should not complain if the new converts are not strong in the spiritual life. We have to criticize ourselves. It is hard for weak parents to bring forth strong children. The health of the children depends very much on the parents. In the matter of gospel preaching, we all have to learn and be dealt with.

I worship the Lord in these days because I realize that not only are the brothers and sisters doing the work of preaching, but they are being dealt with by the Lord and learning the lessons. If a brother quarrels with someone, can he go out after that to preach the gospel? If a brother lies to someone during the day, can he preach the gospel in the evening? His power will be gone, and his mouth will be shut up by his lie. His conscience knows, and the evil spirit knows. When he goes to open his mouth to testify for Jesus, the enemy will say, "You are a liar," and his mouth will be shut. In order to preach, you have to confess your sins. You have to deal with your lies, and you have to be dealt with by the Lord in this very specific matter. Then your conscience will be clean. You will have the freedom, and you will have the boldness to say something for Christ.

To preach the gospel requires us to be dealt with. It is easy to be used by the Lord to speak a word of edification, but it is not easy to speak a word of preaching. If you are going to preach the gospel, you have to be dealt with by the Lord. How can you help someone to repent with a 180 degree turn if you do not turn in this way? It is impossible to have only a 45 degree turn and ask people to have a 180 degree turn. If we ourselves have not turned to such a degree, how can we help people to repent? However, if we cannot help people to turn 180 degrees back to God, we have done a poor job of preaching. We have to help people to have a full, thorough repentance toward God.

Many people when they repented have said, "Lord, from this day my thoughts turn to You. My family life turns to You. My business, my job, my schooling, my friendships, even my driving, and everything turn to You. Whatever I have, whatever I do, whatever I can do, and whatever I am, I turn all these to You." As a person believing in Christ, you have to do this. Otherwise, something dirty or sinful in the eyes of God still remains in you. That poisons the Christian life. You have to clear up what you have been, what you have been doing, and how you have been living. This is a real and thorough repentance.

This kind of repentance is an uprooting. It uproots you from this sinful world. Our life and living have been too rooted in this sinful world. Now we have to uproot our living out of this world. Real repentance is an uprooting out of this earth, out of this sinful world. We need such a repentance toward God, and we need to help others to realize such a repentance.

## A THOROUGH CONFESSION OF SINS

Following repentance, you need to make a confession of your sins. You have to confess all your sins before God. First John 1:9 says, "If we confess our sins, He is faithful and righteous to forgive us our sins and cleanse us from all unrighteousness." This forgiving, this cleansing, depends on our confession. We have to make a thorough confession.

Someone may ask what sins are. This is a real problem. How can we define sins? Verse 4 of chapter three says, "Everyone who practices sin practices lawlessness also, and sin is lawlessness." What is sin? Sin is to transgress the law, to break the law. Any kind of transgression of the law is sin. In the Scriptures there is the law, which includes not only the Ten Commandments but many bylaws and regulations. The Ten Commandments do not tell us to love our neighbor as ourselves, but this is an item of the regulations with the law; it is a part of the law. If you do not love others, you are breaking the law. This is a sin. Any kind of transgression of the law is sin.

In the Ten Commandments there is a commandment that says we must honor our parents. Have you always honored your parents? Do not think that as an old person I am condemning the young generation, but I do realize that today's generation is wrong in this matter. Sometimes teenage children tell their parents, "You are too old. You do not know what is right; I do." To take this kind of attitude toward your parents is sin, because it is a transgression of the law.

In the Ten Commandments there is another commandment that tells us we should not steal. Someone may say that he never steals from others. I do not believe you have never stolen. In actuality, you have stolen many times. Many students steal answers in order to pass their examinations. Some children even steal from their parents. There is no need for me to go into detail. You know all the stories better than I do. All those are sins. Any kind of transgression of the law is sin.

First John 5:17a says, "All unrighteousness is sin." Unrighteousness and injustice are sin. If you are not righteous and just, that is sin. In this country, in the Far East, and in Europe, many people are not just and righteous when they go to the market. They try to get more than what they pay for. I present this simple definition to you. What is sin? Sin is the transgression of law. Sin is unrighteousness. Anything unjust and unrighteous is sin.

In order to be a proper believer in Christ, you have to confess all your sins; you must make a thorough confession. You may not consider that you are sinful, but if you desire to take care of this need, go to spend some time with the Lord. You now proclaim that you believe in Jesus, and you have made the decision for Christ. That is good. Praise the Lord! Since this is so, spend some time with the Lord. Consider all your relationships—with your parents, your wife, your husband, your children, and your schoolmates, roommates, friends, and relatives. While you are considering all these relationships, the Holy Spirit may come to you and say, "You are wrong with your parents in a certain matter. Ten years ago you were wrong in certain things with your father. You are wrong with your schoolmates, wrong with your neighbors, wrong with this man, and wrong with that man." In addition, when many Christians check all the material things in their possession, they will find out how many sinful things they have. In order to be a living, proper believer in Christ, you need to have such a dealing, such a confession to confess all your sins before God.

When we go to help others, we have to pray much. We ourselves first have to be cleansed by confession. Then we will have the ground and will be in the atmosphere to help people to realize their need for cleansing. By the grace and the anointing of the Holy Spirit, we will be able to help people to realize that they need this kind of confession. Why are so many Christians dead? It is because they have so many old sins. The old sins still remain within them. They have to confess all those things away. Every believer needs a confession of all his sinful things before God and a clearance of his whole life.

## CONFESSING THE LORD JESUS BEFORE MEN

Believers also need another kind of confession, not only the confession of sins but the confession of the Lord. They have to confess the Lord Jesus before men. From now on you must confess, you must tell others, that you belong to the Lord. Now you have become a Christian, a believer. Confess the name of the Lord Jesus, and confess before men that Jesus is the Lord and your Savior. Romans 10:9 says, "That if you confess with your mouth Jesus as Lord and believe in your heart that God has raised Him from the dead, you will be saved." We confess Jesus as the Lord with our mouth.

It is very strange that throughout the whole earth—in the East and in the West, in Europe and in Asia—people have a feeling of shame when confessing Christ. If someone says, "Now I believe Christ; I confess Jesus is Lord," there is to some degree the feeling of shame. It is also very strange that when people follow Confucius and tell others about it, they have a feeling not of shame but of boldness. This sin of shame comes from the devil, Satan. We have to fight the battle by the grace and mercy of God to overcome this feeling of shame. Sometimes in the past I told Satan, "Satan if you keep giving me this feeling of shame, I will shout my confession." The devil is frightened by this, and he runs away.

The proper believing in the Lord Jesus includes the step of telling people that from this day you are no more an unbeliever. From today you are a believer in Jesus. You have received Jesus as your Savior and as your Lord. From this day you confess that He is the Lord and that you belong to Him. After you believe in the Lord Jesus, you need to go back to tell your parents, relatives, friends, and neighbors and make a thorough confession of Christ. Young students, after you believe in Christ, you should go to your schoolmates to tell them, "Now I am different. Yesterday I was without Christ, but today Christ is within me."

There is a need for a real repentance and two different kinds of confessions: the confession of sins before God and the confession of Jesus Christ as Lord before men. You should not try to be a hidden Christian, a secret Christian, or a nice Christian within but with no appearance without. Learn to be released by the confession of Christ before men. In China I saw certain brothers do something very interesting. You may say that this was too much, but if you were in that environment, you would realize that there was the need for it. After they were saved, some brothers put a label on their clothing that said, "I am a Christian today." In many cases that helped them. Others would say, "Do not go to him for certain matters, because he is a Christian. Do not try to convince him, because he is a Christian. Do not ask him to play certain games or go to the movies with you, because he is a Christian." In order to be a living, prevailing, powerful believer, you have to make a public confession of Christ before people.

## BEING BAPTIZED

You also have to be baptized. To be baptized means to be buried. After you believe in the Lord Jesus, right away you have to be buried, because you realize that you are so sinful, good for nothing but death. You realize that you have been crucified with Christ on the cross, so you are dead already. You have been dead for two thousand years. Since you realize that you are dead, you must be willing for the church to give you a funeral, to bury you. This is very necessary.

From my youth I was raised in a semi-Christian home. I heard many stories of the gospel, and I was educated and brought up in a Christian school. However, it was not until I was nineteen years old that I was saved. Before that day I knew many things about Christianity. I knew almost all the stories about Jesus in the four Gospels. We were taught these things in the Sunday Schools. Sometimes we would even make jokes about those stories. However, when I was nineteen years old, I experienced a real salvation. On that day I realized that I was sinful and that with me there was no good thing. Within me, every bit is evil. I did not like myself; I hated myself. I realized that this man is good for nothing and that he must truly be buried.

As a member of a so-called church, however, I already had been baptized by sprinkling. At that time I had not repented, and I had not believed or prayed. I had not realized that I was a sinner, and I had not truly known that Christ was my Savior. I only knew something about Christ. Nevertheless, the pastor told me I had to be sprinkled. He told the congregation, "This young man is a member of a Christian family, with a very nice mother and sister. Therefore, we have to sprinkle him." This kind of sprinkling did not mean anything. Later when I was saved, I realized that I was a dead person, good for nothing, and that I had to be buried. I was anxious to be buried, so I went to some Christians who loved the Lord. I asked them, "Is it right that I have to be baptized? I have already been sprinkled." They told me it was one hundred percent right for me to be baptized. I said, "Then we had better do it right away. Bury me!" After you believe in the Lord Jesus, if you seek the Lord within you, there will be the desire to be baptized, to be buried.

In a certain place a small native boy became a member of the Catholic Church. The Catholic Church did not allow people to eat meat on Friday, but they allowed people to eat fish. One Friday the little boy went out to hunt, brought home a deer, and began to cook it. While it was cooking, a priest passed the house and smelled the meat, so he came to the door and scolded him. That little boy had been given the name of Johnny. He said, "A few years ago I was not named Johnny. I had a native name, but one day you brought me to your church and sprinkled me. From that time you told me, 'That is no longer your name; now you are Johnny.' This morning I went out and tried to catch fish. I could not catch any, but I took a deer, sprinkled it, and said, 'You are no longer a deer; you are now a fish.' I believed what you told me, so why do you not believe what I am telling you?" We do not baptize people in this false way, to put some water on them and change their name. Rather, to be baptized means that you realize that you are dead with Christ and in Christ. Now you are allowing the church to bury you by putting you into the water. Friends, after you believe in Christ, you need to be baptized. You cannot baptize yourself; you must be baptized.

## BEING FILLED AND BAPTIZED WITH THE HOLY SPIRIT

You must also receive the Holy Spirit, be filled with the Spirit, and be baptized in the Spirit. As the third Person of the Triune God, the Holy Spirit is the very transmission of God to you. In order to receive Christ, to receive God, you have to receive the Holy Spirit. The Holy Spirit is nothing less than Christ Himself. Today the Holy Spirit is waiting for you, so you have to open yourself. After you thoroughly repent, make a thorough confession of sins, make a prevailing confession of Christ before men, and are willing to be baptized, you have the ground to claim the infilling and the outpouring of the Holy Spirit. When we preach the gospel, we have to preach to such an extent that we tell people, "You are entitled to receive the Holy Spirit." Simply take my word and put it into practice. I believe the Holy Spirit will honor you and honor your practice.

Acts 2:38 says, "And Peter said to them, Repent and each one of you be baptized upon the name of Jesus Christ for the forgiveness of your sins, and you will receive the gift of the Holy Spirit." This verse says first to repent, second to be baptized, and third to receive the gift of the Holy Spirit. These are three of the five practices that we have mentioned in this message. In addition, following repentance and before being baptized you need two confessions, the confession of sins before God and the confession of the Lord Jesus before men. To be baptized is also a kind of confession, a silent but public confession not only to men but also to the entire universe, to the heavens and to the earth, that today you are in Christ and buried with Christ. Then you are entitled, you have the ground to claim, the gift of the Holy Spirit.

All that God is and all that Christ has done—all this goodness, all the blessings, and all the items of the salvation of God—are in the Holy Spirit. Through a process, the Holy Spirit now includes God, Christ, salvation, and all the goodness of salvation. You have to be filled with this Holy Spirit. After you repent, confess your sins before God, confess Christ as your Lord before men, and are baptized, right away you are entitled to, you are on the ground to claim, the gift of the Holy Spirit. When you are going to be baptized, you have to say, "Lord, today is the very day that I claim the fullness of the Holy Spirit." Claim it and take it. If you have not been baptized yet, but you have the desire to be baptized, in the eyes of God it is as if you have been baptized already. Now you can stand on this ground and claim the Holy Spirit, telling the Lord, "Lord, You have to fill me with the Holy Spirit, and You have to pour out the Holy Spirit upon me. This is my entitlement, and this is my portion." You have to claim this.

In our preaching we have to help people to realize these five steps: to repent thoroughly, to confess their sins before God, to make a confession publicly before men, to be baptized, and to realize that after they do this, they are entitled to the fullness of the Holy Spirit. I say again, we are not here telling people to receive a certain kind of religion. We are here learning how to help people to realize this living Christ. This living Christ today is the Spirit. He is not a religion; He is a living Person. It is not Christianity; it is Christ Himself as the Spirit. How can you receive the Spirit with this living Christ? It is by repenting, confessing your sins, confessing Christ as the Lord, and being baptized. If you are willing to do these four things, you are on the ground and entitled to claim the gift of the Holy Spirit. This is wonderful! Then you will be a living Christian. We do ask the Lord to reveal Himself to the dear new ones, that they all will have a living contact, a living touch, with the Lord and that the Lord will reveal Himself to them that they may know Christ within them in a living way.

CHAPTER SEVEN

## PREACHING THE GOSPEL
## AS THE VITAL AND ULTIMATE GOAL
## OF OUR CHRISTIAN LIVING

Scripture Reading: Acts 1:8; Phil. 1:5, 27

Acts 1:8 says, "But you shall receive power when the Holy Spirit comes upon you, and you shall be My witnesses both in Jerusalem and in all Judea and Samaria and unto the uttermost part of the earth." I would like to stress the word *witnesses*. Here *witnesses* in Greek does not refer to testimonies but to persons. "You shall be My witnesses" means "you shall be My living, witnessing persons." Philippians 1:5 says, "For your fellowship unto the furtherance of the gospel from the first day until now," and verse 27 says, "Only, conduct yourselves in a manner worthy of the gospel of Christ, that whether coming and seeing you or being absent, I may hear of the things concerning you, that you stand firm in one spirit, with one soul striving together along with the faith of the gospel."

The church of Christ is on the earth today to fight the battle for the kingdom of God, that is, to subdue the enemy and to plunder his goods. His goods are souls, the sinners and people of the world. Satan has usurped this earth, especially by keeping the worldly people in his hand. First John 5:19 tells us that the whole world lies in the hand of the evil one. *World,* as used by the Holy Spirit in the Gospel of John and the Epistle of John, refers to the worldly people. The worldly people today are under the hand of the evil one, the usurping hand of the devil. Therefore, on the earth during the New Testament dispensation there is a real battle between God and Satan, a battle over people's souls. To fight the battle, subdue the enemy, and set free all the souls under his usurping hand is the main purpose for the church's being on this earth. However, we must realize that this is different from the so-called evangelizing work of Christianity. To subdue the enemy Satan and to release people from his usurping hand is one thing; to evangelize people is another thing. The word *evangelize* is good, but its meaning is not completely right.

## KNOWING AND EXPERIENCING CHRIST AS LIFE

For the proper church life, there are always five things that we must have in a balanced way: life, light and truth, the church, service, and ultimately the preaching of the gospel. The first item is life. We must know Christ as our inner life, take Him as our life, and experience Him as our life. This is the basic matter, the foundation.

## KNOWING THE TRUTH

Second, we need the truth, the knowledge, of the Scriptures to balance the inner life. This is like a train, which runs on two tracks. It is dangerous for a train to run on only one track. Two tracks are necessary for a train to run in a proper way. Likewise, we need the track of life and the track of truth. This is why we spend much time to study the Word. The Word affords and supplies us not only with the life supply but also with light. Life is within, and light is without. We pay our attention not only to life but also to light. We may also compare this to our physical body, which needs energy within and the light without. If we are full of energy within but are in darkness, we would do many things wrongly; the more we would do, the more we would be wrong. If we have both the energy within and the light without, then the more we do, the better. We need life, and we need light. The light is the truth in the Scriptures. Therefore, every balanced, normal Christian must have abundant life within and must have adequate knowledge, truth, and light from the Word. This is why every one of us must be trained in and with the Word.

## LIVING IN THE CHURCH, THE BODY OF CHRIST

Third, we need the church life. In these past years we have

seen many people who pay their attention to the inner life and the light of truth, but they neglect the church life. There are not only the two aspects of life and light; we also need the other three aspects: the Body, the service, and the gospel. We are members of the Body, so we need the church life. We might have abundant life and adequate light, but if we are not living in the Body, in the church, we are disembodied. We are isolated members. An isolated member is a dead member. We may be dead because of isolation from the Body.

## SERVING IN THE BODY

Fourth, we need to function, to serve, in the Body. As members of the church, we must realize what our function is and what kind of members we are. Do you have any member in your physical body which does not function? If someone's foot does not function, it becomes a burden to him. If we do not function, we become a burden to the Body of Christ. Others have to carry us. We may even be incurably sick to such an extent that we are cut off. The Lord mentioned this kind of cutting off in John 15:6, which says, "If one does not abide in Me, he is cast out as a branch and is dried up." To be cast out as a branch is to be cut off from the Body. We need to function, to serve.

## PREACHING TO SUBDUE THE ENEMY
## AND PLUNDER HIS GOODS

The main item of the service in the church is the work of preaching. As the Body, what are we living here for? We are here for the purpose of fighting the battle to subdue the enemy, to bring people back to God. This is not a kind of evangelizing work in Christianity. It is the testimony of the church, and all the members are the living witnesses. With these members there is a testimony, and this testimony is in the genuine preaching. The real preaching of the church is the living of the members. All the members live for this purpose. Their living is their preaching.

We have to know the Lord as our life within, we need to have adequate light from the Word, we must be in the church, and we have to function as living members in the church.

In this way we become a living Body always cooperating and coordinating together in order to subdue the enemy and release the souls. To release the souls is the ultimate goal of our service. This is not merely a preaching work; this is the vital and ultimate goal of our Christian living.

## THE PREACHING OF THE GOSPEL
## NOT BEING A WORK BUT A LIVING

For what purpose are we living here? It is to defeat the enemy and release the souls from his hand. In Matthew 12:29 the Lord said, "Or how can anyone enter into the house of the strong man and plunder his goods unless he first binds the strong man? And then he will thoroughly plunder his house." The strong man is Satan, and his goods are living persons. We have to plunder his house and release his goods; we must release the precious souls out of his hand. Again it seems that this is just the evangelizing work of Christianity. In actuality, though, it is very different. This is not merely a work; it is a living. We are living for gospel preaching.

All these words are right—*evangelize, gospel, preaching*—but they are inaccurately used by today's Christianity. Christianity takes the evangelizing work simply as a work, an activity, a kind of program. The New Testament, however, shows us that gospel preaching must be a kind of living. This is our life. We are living here for this. Preaching is our life and living. Why are you living here? If you say you are living to study at college, you are wrong. As a Christian you are not living to study. Rather, you are studying for your living of preaching. Therefore, you have to preach in your school, not only by your word but also by your conduct, your living, and your work.

You have to speak. Some people say that we should not speak too much. However, you have to speak much. The more you speak the better. If you speak ten thousand words, and only one word is received by others, that is a profit. It is better than nothing. The Communists train their people to speak for their cause. However, if you study human history, you can see that preaching, or "propaganda," was invented by the church. Do you know how the newspaper was invented? It was invented to a great extent by the Reformation. The reformers were the first to use newspapers for the purpose of preaching. Regrettably, today's Christianity has lost this inheritance, and the enemy, the devil, and the worldly people have picked the newspaper up to utilize it. The church is far behind in this matter. We have to "propagandize"; we have to preach. Preaching is the invention of the church. We lost it, but now we have to recover it. Therefore, go out to preach.

To be a living person who preaches the gospel, you have to preach with your mouth, ears, eyes, nose, two hands, and two feet. With your two hands you have to write, and with your two feet you have to travel. We have to use our whole being for preaching. We are living preachers, not professional preachers. If you know God's economy, then you realize that the purpose for the church's being on this earth is preaching, and this preaching is not merely an evangelizing work. It is the living of all the living members of the Body. The whole Body, with all the living members, lives for the purpose of subduing the enemy, releasing the souls, bringing them to Christ, and building the Body with these persons as the materials.

## THE CHURCH'S NEED FOR NEW ONES

History tells us the real situation. I have been on this earth for many years. I have been a genuine Christian for more than forty years, and I have been in this work for more than thirty-five years. Just within the past two decades I have seen many groups in the Far East, in Europe, and in this country. I speak the truth that you can never have a living group of Christians serving the Lord in an adequate way without these five aspects to balance them: life, light, the church, service, and ultimately preaching. I saw some groups that were rich in life but poor in knowledge. I also saw some groups, and I was with one of them, that were rich in knowledge. One person among them was known as a "living concordance." They were rich in knowledge, but they were very poor in life. In the past I have known some groups that were rich both in life and in knowledge, but they were poor in the church life, so they did not last long. Some groups even proclaim that they are rich in life, rich in knowledge, and also have the church life, but they are short of gospel preaching. After five years passed there were still the same number meeting with them, and after another five years there was no increase. They always said, "The Lord is with us. This is wonderful!" They were wonderful for ten years but still with the same people. Eventually in their twelfth year they lost their interest and disbanded. I saw this in 1957 and again in 1963. In another example, I recently received a letter saying that a group that had been meeting for more than twenty years also lost their interest and disbanded. They said, "What are we doing here? Year after year we have the same people."

In a family with only a wife and husband, the first five years are wonderful. Then the next five, even up to twenty years, are still wonderful. After twenty-five years, however, they will not feel very wonderful. They need some children, some "new ones." In the same way, the church needs some new ones. In order for the church to be strong, you have to have normal deliveries, normal births. If next week fifty persons are baptized, the whole church will be on fire. On the one hand, I was happy to see several people receive the Lord in a recent gospel meeting. Some may wonder how so many people could confess the Lord Jesus in just one meeting. On the other hand, in the past I have seen one thousand people stand up to acknowledge the Lord's name. It is good for a few people to receive the Lord, but according to my experience, this seems like two drops of water. Still, though, the brothers and sisters are excited. Some proclaim, "This is wonderful, wonderful!" However, if you would endeavor, pray, and work to bring more people in, next week you may baptize fifty, one hundred fifty, or two hundred people. Then you will be so excited that you will not care to eat. I saw this in the past. The church needs new births, new deliveries. The church needs new ones.

Whenever there is such a suggestion to preach the gospel, the spirit of all the saints responds. The Holy Spirit within the spirit of the saints honors this, because this is the purpose of God in this age on the earth. However, the church has lost sight of this matter, so now we have to recover this. We have to realize what we are doing here. Are we here only to meet together and to have a wonderful message meeting on the

Lord's Day morning and a wonderful Lord's table meeting in the evening? Are we here to have a wonderful prayer meeting on Wednesday and a study meeting on Friday, and then do it again the next week, the next month, and the next year? There is no need for five years to pass; even within this year if you would not bring in more people, someone will eventually say that there is no need for us to come together. There will be disappointment among us.

## TAKING PREACHING AS OUR LIVING

We need the proper preaching as the very living of the church. This is not a work; it is a living. We are living here for this. We must do it not just once for our whole life; rather, it must be a regular matter. I do not like to speak much about the church in Taipei, but I can testify that after many years of building up, the church there has been brought to this normal condition. They are living there for this purpose. Day by day they are growing, day by day they are being built up, and month after month a good number of people are brought into the church.

From now on we all have to learn that to preach the gospel is our living. It is for this very purpose that we are living here. We have to labor on people. As a student you have to work on your classmate and your roommate. As a man working in a business, you have to work on your colleague. You have to work on your neighbors, your relatives, and the persons whom you know. This is our living. We must always live for this.

This prevailing preaching depends on life, truth, the church, and service. If you have these four items, then you will have a strong standing and a prevailing preaching. Do not think that our preaching was only in the past. Rather, that was only a start. From now on, we must take preaching as our living. Week after week, month after month, and year after year we are living here for this—to win the world for Christ and win souls for Christ. In order to do this, we have to be filled with Christ, we have to have light, we have to be in the church, and we have to be functioning members. Then we will be prevailing in our preaching.

This is the third time that I have been in this country, and

I have been here for more than three years. Many Christian friends told me that I should not and cannot compare the situation here in the United States with that of Taiwan. In a sense I agree with this, but in another sense I do not agree. It depends on how much the church lives for preaching and labors for it. If we brothers and sisters all would work in this way, we will see the difference. We have seen some difference already, but I believe that this is just a small start. We have to fight the battle to create the atmosphere of gospel preaching in the church. We should let the community know that we are a group of people living here for people's souls. I say again, this is our living. This is the basic understanding of preaching the gospel.

## THE NEED TO COORDINATE
## IN OUR WORK WITH PEOPLE

We should keep a record of the persons who are interested in receiving the Lord or already have made a decision for Christ. These are the materials we have to work on. This is the opportunity for us to be coordinated practically, like a team that plays ball. We have to work on these dear ones in a coordinated way. A young sister in school may have two or three classmates that have the desire to believe in Christ. For her to work with them by herself is not adequate; it will not be powerful and prevailing. She needs to coordinate with one or two other sisters. Then the three can work together on these classmates, and within two weeks they all will be saved. They will be saved thoroughly, not only to know Christ but also to know the church. In turn, these three sisters may have some relatives who also are close to believing. It may be hard for them to work with their relatives, so a brother may have to coordinate with them. When these four coordinate together, it will be easy to bring in all those relatives. To keep your relatives and friends in your own hands will be hard for you, and to keep my relatives and friends in my own hands will be hard for me. However, if we coordinate, it will be easy to fight the battle in the Body in a coordinated way.

Learn the lesson to coordinate. There is no need to be proud. To be proud is the most foolish way to do things. You may say, "I can do everything. I do not need these poor sisters to help me. I know everything from Genesis to Revelation, and I know how to save souls. I have been trained." However, if you go to play ball by yourself without a team, how can you win the game? You need the coordination. Learn to be coordinated. Trust in the Lord, and trust in the Body. Whatever you cannot get through, bring this matter to the Body. When you cannot fight the battle, ask the brothers and sisters to come and help. Learn to ask people to come in to coordinate. Then you will see the effect. This is a spiritual law. When you throw something into the air, it falls again because of the law of gravity. You cannot get around a law. If you ask others to come in, you will be right. Try this. The enemy, the devil and the evil spirits, know the secret. They are not afraid of you as an individual, but if you call one or two brothers to come along with you, the evil spirits will be afraid. Always work two by two, not one by one. Learn to be coordinated together.

Two brothers can keep the records on file for the men who are new ones, and two sisters can keep the records for the women. These two brothers must be diligent. They have to read and study the records with prayer to know their situation. They may consider that a certain brother should coordinate with the one who contacted a new one. This will be a great help. Then that brother can report on his contact with the new one, and if there is a certain difficult situation, a third brother can be brought in to reinforce the other two. Now instead of two, these three will go to work on this person. Those who coordinate in this way will study the situations of the new ones. Then they may call on other brothers and sisters to coordinate with them. Do not say that you do not know how to do this. I know that you do not know how to do it, but do it by learning. It is by doing it that you learn how. If you never do it, you will never know how to do it. Take the assignment and limitation given to you. Just like a member of a ball team, you cannot say, "Don't give me the ball." Whether or not you are ready, the ball will come to you. You have to play, because you all are in the game. Do not say you are too busy. Learn to accept the responsibility. Then I assure you that you will receive the blessing—not only the blessing in others' salvation, but also in your own growth of life.

## PRODUCING A HARVEST
## BY PREACHING THE GOSPEL IN LIFE

The new ones who come in will bring in more new ones. The situation with the old members is too settled. Consider the fruit trees. It is not the old branches that bear the fruit; it is the new branches. This is why growers cut off the old branches; it is to produce new branches. With the new branches there is more possibility of bearing fruit. If the new ones bring in more new ones, the work of preaching will always be spreading. Then we will have a farm and a garden, something we have grown, and it will constantly produce. It is in this way, the way of the church preaching the gospel, that people will be brought in. Then after they are brought in, they will do the same thing we do in the same way. I am happy for our small start. I cannot predict how far this will go, but a living grain of wheat that falls into the earth reproduces thirty, sixty, or a hundred grains. Then the second harvest will be bigger, and the third harvest will be even bigger.

On the one hand, the responsible brothers and sisters may ask you to coordinate with certain ones, but on the other hand, there is no need for you to wait. Do not say you have not been assigned yet. Forget about this. If you have some relatives, you may right away ask another brother to help you work on them. Do not make anything a legality. There is only one legality, that is, to save people. As long as we are living here for the Lord to subdue the enemy and plunder his goods for the Lord, we are right, and we will receive the blessing.

The primary matter is not preaching; it is the building up. The primary issue of preaching the gospel is the building up of the Body; the secondary issue is the preaching itself. It is in this way that we will be built up as a building and in the Spirit be formed as an army to fight the battle. The Lord has given us a small but living start. We will see harvest after harvest; we will see many times of producing. This is a matter of life. It is not merely an activity or a movement. Rather, it is something living.

## TAKING THE POWER FROM ON HIGH
## ON THE STANDING OF THE BODY

In order to be prevailing, each one of us must deal with the Lord and be dealt with by Him. You must have a thorough dealing with the Lord to consecrate yourselves once again and to claim the Lord's richness and fullness. Day by day, whenever you contact people, you have to say, "Lord, I am a member standing on the ground of the Body." You must not only claim the power from on high but take it. There is no need merely to claim it. Take it! It is yours. Hold it, and share in it. Every day when you are going out to contact people, have this kind of prevailing prayer. There is no need to pray behind closed doors. While you are on your way driving, you can say, "Lord, I am going out as a member on the ground of the Body. I take the power from on high by faith." The Lord always honors faith. The more you do not have any evidence, yet still believe, the more the Lord will honor you and honor your faith. You will see the blessing of power in the result, and even you yourselves will be surprised. You will hardly be able to believe what happens.

We all have to learn to live, work, and act in faith. Before you believe, however, you have to be dealt with. Your conscience has to be cleansed and purged. You have to deal with the Lord and be dealt with by Him. If there is something accusing your conscience, faith will not work. Learn this lesson. Put all these things into practice, and you will see the results. This will produce more and more fruit.

# Chapter Eight

## THE FELLOWSHIP UNTO
## THE FURTHERANCE OF THE GOSPEL

Scripture Reading: Phil. 1:5-6, 12, 18-20, 27

In the books written by the apostle Paul, only Philippians speaks in a particular way concerning the preaching of the gospel. Philippians 1:5 says, "For your fellowship unto the furtherance of the gospel from the first day until now." Paul opens this book with his prayer in which he joyfully thanks the Lord that the Philippians are in the fellowship unto the furtherance of the gospel. Here the apostle used the word *fellowship* instead of *preaching*. This is very meaningful. To speak merely of the preaching of the gospel is a little shallow, but to speak of the fellowship unto the furtherance of the gospel is very deep. We Christians today may not know clearly what it means to have the fellowship unto the furtherance of the gospel.

Many Bible students recognize that the church in Philippi was a church that preached the gospel. The apostle Paul prayed for them that their fellowship unto the furtherance of the gospel might be carried on to work out God's purpose. In verse 6 he continues, "Being confident of this very thing, that He who has begun in you a good work will complete it until the day of Christ Jesus." Through this prayer we can realize that God's intention is that a local church would have the fellowship unto the furtherance of the gospel, not only for one period of time but continually, until the day of the Lord Jesus Christ, that is, until He comes back. In reading this word we can also realize that the apostle was burdened that this fellowship would not be interrupted. Therefore, he said he was confident that He who had begun in them a good work would complete it until the day of His coming back. By this we can see that there is a real battle. God's intention is to have the local churches in the fellowship unto the further-ance of the gospel, but there is the possibility that this fellowship, which is a good work begun by the Lord Himself, might be interrupted. I have the sense and the burden that it is right to apply this word to us. A good work has begun among us, but there is the possibility that it will be inter-rupted; it may be stopped. Therefore, we have to pray that the Lord will keep this work going on and on until the day of His coming back.

Paul told the Philippians that his imprisonment would also work to the advancement of the gospel. Verses 12 and 18 say, "Now I want you to know, brothers, that the things concerning me have turned out rather to the advancement of the gospel....What then? Only that in every way, whether in pretense or in truthfulness, Christ is announced; and in this I rejoice; yes, and I will rejoice." Even his being in prison was a kind of furtherance of the gospel.

He also said that while he was imprisoned, he had the desire, the burden, to magnify Christ. Verse 20 says, "Accord-ing to my earnest expectation and hope that in nothing I will be put to shame, but with all boldness, as always, even now Christ will be magnified in my body, whether through life or through death." This tells us that the genuine preaching of the gospel is not merely the preaching of the word, but a life of magnifying Christ.

Then at the end of this chapter, he tells us that we must have a kind of conduct, a daily walk and living, that becomes the gospel of Christ. Verse 27a says, "Only, conduct yourselves in a manner worthy of the gospel of Christ, that whether coming and seeing you or being absent, I may hear of the things concerning you." We must have a life, a conversation, a walk, which corresponds with our gospel. Then verse 27b says, "That you stand firm in one spirit, with one soul striving together along with the faith of the gospel." The word *strive* here means to labor, to fight. We have to labor, fight, and strive together. The word *together* is also very meaningful, having the sense of "as one man, shoulder to shoulder in absolute cooperation." This requires that we be in one spirit and with one mind.

## THE GENUINE PREACHING OF THE GOSPEL BEING A FELLOWSHIP

There are a number of matters in these verses that I am burdened to pass on to you so that you may put them into practice. First, we must learn that the preaching of the gospel is a matter not merely of individuals. It is a matter of the Body. In verse 5 the apostle Paul uses the word *fellowship,* speaking of the fellowship unto the furtherance of the gospel. If this were a matter of individuals only, there would be no need for fellowship. The move of the preaching of the gospel must be a matter in fellowship, because it is a matter of the Body.

John 15 tells us that all the branches bear fruit (vv. 1-5). A tree has not only one branch; it has many branches, and all the branches bear fruit in a way of fellowship. This is why later in that chapter the Lord Jesus tells us that we have to love one another (vv. 12, 17). If we love one another, the people of the world will see that we are the disciples of Christ (13:34-35). If we preach Christ yet do not have fellowship and do not love one another, our fruit will be very limited; we will not be very fruitful. In order to be fruitful, we have to love one another. This is the strongest testimony to the unbelievers.

All people deep within are seeking a life and love in real mutuality. This desire for mutuality is in the human nature as something created by God. Not one human being truly wants to live by himself or herself individually. However, because of the damage done by the evil one, there is no real mutuality among humanity and in human society. There is no mutuality in life, in love, in truth, and in sincerity. If we Christian brothers, however, live together in pure love and sincerity, this will become a strong testimony. This sincere, pure love lived out by us is the very life of Christ. This love is Christ expressed through us. When we live by Christ, in Christ, with Christ, and for Christ, we have love for one another, and this mutual love becomes a strong testimony.

This is the outworking of the inner life and the power to bear fruit.

In order to be prevailing and fruitful in the preaching of the gospel, we must pay our full attention to the Body life. The more we live in the Body life and have the reality of the Body life, the more we will be fruitful. Such a life will be a strong testimony to our relatives, friends, schoolmates, and neighbors. When all these people see the kind of mutual love we have among us as Christian brothers, they will be very impressed and influenced. This will pave the way and open the door for the Holy Spirit to work in their hearts. To have the real Body life helps us to be prevailing. I believe that this is the very reason why the apostle Paul uses the word *fellowship* in Philippians 1:5. All the branches bear fruit together, one with another. Not one branch bears fruit individually.

In preaching the gospel, we have to learn the Body life. By this kind of preaching we will be built up together more and more. If we are burdened for a neighbor, we will ask some brothers to help us bring this neighbor to the Lord. If we are burdened for a classmate, we will ask some others to help us bring this classmate to the Lord. We will work not just by ourselves, but we will invite the brothers to work together with us in a way of coordination. I say again, if we have the spirit of the Body life, people will sense it. If we have love among us, people around us will sense what we have, and that love and living will be a very strong factor to convince the unbelievers—our neighbors and friends—to open their spirits to the Lord. We need the Body life, and the best way to be built up together is for us to have the fellowship unto the furtherance of the gospel.

It may be hard to bring a certain relative to the Lord, but we can invite him to our home and on the same night also invite three or four brothers and sisters. Then we can work together on this relative. However, this must not be merely an outward activity. If we do not have the mutual love and the reality of the Body life, even if we invite three or four to come, they will bring only coldness. They will not bring warmth, and there will be no reality. If on the other hand, we are in the

Body life and we have the reality, nothing will be able to conceal that reality. When three or four brothers and sisters come to our home, there will be the influence; there will be something that warms people. People will realize that among these Christians there is something very special, something quite attractive. We must have this kind of love.

The more we go on to have the preaching of the gospel, the more we will be built up together. We will be thoroughly joined and knit together. This will be a strong testimony, not only to man but also to the principalities and powers in the heavens. This will be a shame to them. We need to learn how to preach the gospel in the fellowship unto the furtherance of the gospel in the Body life. This too is neglected by today's Christianity. Many Christians today think that to preach the gospel is a matter of the individual. Someone may say, "Since I love the Lord, I preach the gospel. That is good enough." This kind of preaching can be prevailing to some extent, but the most prevailing and fruitful way to work in the gospel is to have the fellowship unto the furtherance of the gospel, to preach the gospel by the Body life and in the Body life.

All the souls, the unbelievers, are still usurped by the principalities and powers in the heavens. Those powers would not give up anyone, so we must fight a battle, not by ourselves individually but by keeping the fellowship in the Body life. How fruitful we are in our preaching depends on how much of the reality of the Body we have. According to Philippians, the genuine, fruitful, and prevailing preaching of the gospel is a kind of fellowship. We have to do the preaching in the Body. If we are out of the Body, we cannot fight the battle, because we are disarmed. We must have the Body. Try it; then you will prove that this is the case.

## THE PREACHING OF THE GOSPEL BEING THE EXPERIENCE AND MAGNIFYING OF CHRIST

Philippians tells us the secret of experiencing Christ. After the book of Romans there are the two Corinthians, and after these are four short books: Galatians, Ephesians, Philippians, and Colossians. These four short books are the deepest books. God's central thought, eternal purpose, and economy are revealed in them more than in all the rest of the sixty-six books of the Bible. Colossians tells us who Christ is and how much Christ is. In order to know who Christ is, you have to study Colossians. In relation to God, Christ is the image of God. In relation to creation, He is many items. In relation to the new creation, He is all the members of the Body. Christ is so much; He is everything. He is life to us, our hope for the future, and all in all. Galatians tells us that this all-inclusive Christ must be experienced by us not merely outwardly but inwardly. Christ is revealed in us, Christ lives in us, and Christ has to be formed in us (1:16; 2:20; 4:19). Then in Philippians, Paul tells us the secret of how to experience this all-inclusive Christ. Finally, Ephesians speaks of the Body, the church. The Body comes into existence from Christ and by Christ as the Head. This can be possible only through our inward experience of Christ according to the secret of experiencing Christ.

The book of Philippians is the unique book that tells us how to experience Christ. The experience of Christ is for the preaching of the gospel, and the preaching of the gospel is the very experience of Christ. In other words, the preaching of the gospel is the expression of Christ. When we express Christ, when we live out Christ, and when Christ is expressed through us, there is the preaching of the gospel. Consider the branches of a tree. The bearing of fruit by the branches is the branches' experience of the tree. When the branches experience the life of the tree, the bearing of fruit eventually comes out. Bearing fruit is the outworking of the inner experience of life. A branch cannot experience the life of the tree without bearing fruit. The more the branches properly experience the life of the tree, the more fruit they will bear. In the same way, the preaching of the gospel is the outworking of Christ experienced by us. If we experience Christ, there is the outworking of this life, that is, the preaching of the gospel.

Paul and Silas were put into prison in Philippi (Acts 16:23-25). The magistrates charged the jailer to keep them securely, so he put them into the inner prison and secured their feet in the stocks. At that time Paul and Silas did not preach. They were simply filled with Christ and filled with the Spirit, and at midnight they sang hymns of praise to the Lord. That was not merely preaching in word; that was the expression of Christ, the outward expression of the inner life. That was a strong example of the genuine preaching of the gospel, and the jailer, the keeper of the prison, was saved. If we put that story together with the writing of the book of Philippians, we can realize what the proper preaching of the gospel is. The proper preaching of the gospel is the very expression of Christ.

Suppose, on the other hand, that these two apostles had merely realized that their responsibility was to preach the gospel. They might have tried to do it with a long face, saying, "We preach that Christ is the Savior. You have to believe in Him. If you do not believe in Him, you will go to Hell." This kind of preaching would not have been prevailing. However, these two apostles did not do this kind of preaching. They were simply experiencing Christ. They were filled with Christ, so they were full of joy and singing. This kind of singing is simply the overflow of the indwelling Christ, that is, the expression of Christ. At that time God shook the prison, and the jailer was also shaken and said, "Sirs, what must I do to be saved?" (v. 30). Then he and his whole household were saved. That was the genuine preaching and the real experience of Christ.

Philippians 1:19 contains the secret to experiencing Christ— the bountiful supply of the Spirit of Jesus Christ. This is not only the Spirit of God but the Spirit of Jesus Christ, and with this Spirit there is the bountiful supply. These two apostles, Paul and Silas, lived in this Spirit and received the supply from the Spirit. Therefore, regardless of what kind of situation, in life or in death, even in suffering and in prison, they magnified Christ. To preach the gospel is to magnify Christ. As we have seen, it is a matter of the Body, but it also depends on the magnifying of the Lord in our life. Wherever we are, in school or at the store, among neighbors or among relatives, there must be the magnifying of Christ in our life. We cannot preach the gospel only by our word. We have to preach the gospel by magnifying Christ. We need to experience Christ within and learn the secret of how to experience Christ; then we will have an overflow of Christ. This overflowing is the real preaching. This will minister Christ to others.

## OUR PREACHING REQUIRING PATIENCE
## AND ENDURANCE

We cannot bring anyone to the Lord merely by good fortune. Rather, the work of preaching the gospel to bring people to the Lord requires much patience. We need to learn Christ as our patience that we may continually fight the battle to preach the gospel. The real preaching is a battle. We should not think that we can bring the gospel to people so easily. The apostle Paul used the phrase *striving together* (v. 27). This indicates that we need patience and endurance. George Müller prayed for a certain person to be saved, but that person was not saved during Müller's lifetime. It was after Müller's death that this one was saved. It is not very easy and quick to bring certain persons to the Lord. It requires a real struggle. We all have to learn this lesson. We cannot do a quick work in the preaching of the gospel. To preach the gospel is to have a harvest, and we cannot have a harvest in a quick way. We have to learn patience.

I was saved in such a way. A brother in the Lord worked on me for a very long time. For a time there seemed to be no result. I was too hardened in my heart, and I made up my mind to not care for what he said to me. I believe that more or less he was disappointed, and at a certain time he stopped coming to see me. However, one day after he stopped coming—although I did not know why—I made up my mind to go to a Christian meeting. That was the result of the work of that brother over a long time. We all have to learn patience in this work. As the members of a local church, we all must have this life of preaching. In this preaching life we should not expect to do things in a quick way. Rather, we have to labor. If we all would labor for a certain period, perhaps for two or three years, the doors will be wide open to us.

This is similar to a business in that we need to build up credit. I have seen this happen. In the north of mainland China, in my hometown, we spent more than eight years trying to build up credit for the gospel. In the first eight years, from 1932 to 1940, we never baptized over forty people at one time. Within those eight years there was a real struggle. By the mercy of the Lord, however, the brothers there did their best to keep preaching all the time. Then around 1940 the results burst out. From that time on, we always baptized one or two hundred people. Families, factories, hospitals, and schools—all the doors—were opened, and it was very prevailing. In Taiwan we spent at least one or two years in this way. By that time we had learned more, and a group of trained persons came over from the mainland to carry on the work. This is why the work that began there went so fast. Eventually, the doors were opened.

Now we are just starting in this country. On the one hand, we need some time to be trained, and on the other hand, we need time to build up credit. We cannot sow a seed tonight and have a harvest tomorrow. That is the behavior of mushrooms. Mushrooms are not the right life; they even damage the genuine life. A tree bears fruit in its time. We have to learn patience and endurance. The neighbors, relatives, colleagues, and schoolmates with whom we are working may not be saved in this year. Some may be saved this month, but some may be saved only after five years. We do not know when they will be saved; only the Lord knows. I cannot explain why this is so, but it is a fact. Some will be saved very quickly, but some will be saved very slowly. We cannot care about that. We must simply go on and believe that gradually some fruit will be brought in. Therefore, we need patience.

## OUR PREACHING REQUIRING MUCH PRAYER

This will be a real test of our prayer life. Do not think that to save a soul is an easy task. It requires a certain kind of prayer. When we pray much for a certain person, that person will be saved. We may compare this to a balance. The person is on one side of the balance, and our prayer is on the other side. The more prayer we add, the more weight we have. The weight of the prayers will balance the person, and he will be saved. There is no such thing as fortune in the preaching of the gospel. We cannot expect fortune. Rather, we have to spend much time to pray, to kneel before the Lord for a certain need. This is a real test.

## NEVER ESTIMATING THE RESULT OF OUR PREACHING

No one can tell what the real result of our gospel preaching will be. The brothers and sisters throughout the centuries who did much work of preaching eventually learned one thing. At first, they liked to estimate, to reckon, what kind of result their work would have, but after going on with the Lord for twenty, thirty, or forty years, they eventually came to the point that they would no longer estimate. This is because the results of our work cannot be clear to us. Strictly speaking, we can never know the result of our work. In our preaching of the gospel we may work on six unbelievers in a diligent way. Eventually, three may be saved, while the other three remain stubborn. We cannot do anything with the stubborn ones, so we may become disappointed. It seems that the first three are wonderful, but that is their condition today. After another fifteen years, they all may become backsliders. Of the second three, however, one may become an apostle, and two will become the most profitable elders. If we would ask them how they were saved, they may say, "The first time I heard the gospel was fifteen years ago. At that time I was very impressed, yet I was too stubborn. However, that impression never left me, and after many years, I was saved."

Out of six persons who are saved, two may be weak and four are strong. After only a few years, though, the four strong ones may be very troublesome in the church, but the two weaker ones will become so living with much spiritual understanding. If we knew these stories, we would never estimate the result of our work. Our responsibility is to work and to pray. As to the result, we must leave this matter to the Lord and to time. I can never forget what C. H. Macintosh said: It will only be in the presence of the Lord one day that we will know the real result of our work. The proper way to work is simply to bear responsibility. Never estimate the result. If you estimate the result, you will be either disappointed or proud. Learn the lesson to fellowship with the Lord, to work for Him, and to work in Him. That is good enough.

## BEING IN ONE SPIRIT AND WITH ONE SOUL

We must learn always to be in one spirit and with one soul with the brothers and sisters. To have one soul, to be joined in soul, and to be like-souled are repeated several times in Philippians (1:27; 2:2, 20). Chapter four speaks of two sisters, Euodias and Syntyche. These two were good sisters, but they had a problem. They were not in one spirit and with one mind. Paul told them to think the same thing in the Lord (v. 2).

Philippians is a book on the experience of Christ, and along with the experience of Christ there is the preaching of the gospel. This book tells us clearly that the preaching of the gospel is a matter of fellowship. In fellowship, the most needful thing is the harmony. You can never play good music on the piano if all the keys are not in harmony. In order to work together shoulder to shoulder there must be harmony. Someone may be an extraordinary ball player, but he is useless if he does not stay in harmony with the team; he even becomes a damage to the team.

There is the need of real harmony, especially in preaching the gospel. The more tender and delicate something is, the more it needs harmony. We especially need harmony in the things of the spirit, because the spirit is tender and delicate. The church life, the Body life, is something in the spirit. Do not think that the preaching of the gospel is merely a kind of activity to be carried out in a rough, crude way. We cannot preach in this way. Rather, preaching the gospel is a matter in the spirit. We must have the tender harmony, not only in one spirit, but also with one mind and soul.

Many people have been brought to the Lord through a certain brother. He is not eloquent in speaking, but many persons have been saved through him. The special characteristic of that brother is that he always keeps the harmony. He opens his home to invite people to come. Then he never speaks, but he invites other brothers to speak. What harmony, meekness, and humility is in his spirit! This paves the way for the Holy Spirit to convince people. If among us there is no harmony, no tenderness and humility, we cannot expect people to be saved.

We simply kill the saving Spirit. I have seen a group of brothers who meet together. They cannot preach much, but they have the harmony in tenderness and humility. Among them there is not much preaching, not even much speaking, but people are saved through them. Preaching the gospel is a matter absolutely in the spirit, not in the mentality and not in argument. Therefore, we need the harmony.

All the foregoing matters require our real practice. We cannot expect something according to our imagination. We cannot expect that today we will do something so successful, and then tomorrow we can forget about it. The preaching of the gospel is a lifelong matter. The word of the prayer of the apostle is that He who has begun in you a good work will complete it until the day of Christ Jesus (1:6). We have to keep going on and on. We must pray that the good work that has begun and been established among us by the Lord would keep going on and on, and that we all will learn the lessons. Not only must we preach the gospel to save others, to bring souls to the Lord, but we ourselves must learn the lessons. Then we will be built up together by the outreach of the gospel.

# CHAPTER NINE

## PREACHING THE GOSPEL IN THE WAY OF LIFE

Scripture Reading: Matt. 24:14; 28:19-20; Acts 1:8; 2 Cor. 12:15

Matthew 24:14 says, "And this gospel of the kingdom will be preached in the whole inhabited earth for a testimony to all the nations, and then the end will come." Verses 19 and 20 of chapter twenty-eight say, "Go therefore and disciple all the nations, baptizing them into the name of the Father and of the Son and of the Holy Spirit, teaching them to observe all that I have commanded you. And behold, I am with you all the days until the consummation of the age." Acts 1:8 says, "But you shall receive power when the Holy Spirit comes upon you, and you shall be My witnesses both in Jerusalem and in all Judea and Samaria and unto the uttermost part of the earth." This verse speaks not of preachers but of witnesses.

We Christians need to realize that preaching the gospel must not be a move or an activity. It must be a part, an aspect, an element, of our Christian living. After we are saved, the Lord leaves us on the earth mainly for the purpose of being His witnesses. However, the word *witness* in Greek has a deeper meaning than we might understand. The word *witness* in Greek is "martyr." It is not related merely to preaching but to testifying, not only by word but by our life and living and even the sacrifice of our life. We need to testify the Lord Jesus to others at a cost, even at the sacrifice of our life.

More or less we have a wrong concept due to our particular background. We may think that to preach is merely a kind of work, move, activity, or movement. Rather, the real preaching and outreach of the gospel must be a part of our daily life, our Christian living. We are living here for this, and our living is preaching. We preach not only by word but by our living. Moreover, we preach not in a light and cheap way but at a cost, even at the cost of our life. We have to sacrifice our life for testifying Christ to others. This is why Acts tells us that the preachers of the gospel are the martyrs of the Lord. We have to be the Lord's martyrs. The apostle Paul told the Corinthians that he was willing to spend and be utterly spent for them, that is, to spend whatever he had and whatever he was (2 Cor. 12:15). This means that he was willing to sacrifice his own life, to pay the price at the cost of his own life. I look to the Lord that our concept would be changed. Do not consider that this is a work, movement, or activity. We have to consider that this is a matter of life, an item of our Christian life. We are living here for this, and our living is our preaching.

## WITNESSING FOR THE LORD
## BEING A MATTER OF LIFE, NOT MIRACLES

When we are indifferent to the preaching of the gospel, we are careless about it. However, once we are stirred by the Lord to pay attention to this matter, we have peculiar ideas. We often have the thought that the gospel should be preached in a powerful and miraculous way. This is not the case. Testifying and witnessing for the Lord are a matter of life. Anything miraculous is not normal. I would not say it is abnormal, but it is strange and special. The normal condition is that we live for the gospel, and the outreach of the gospel is the main part of our living.

Many Christians pick up the verses from the Word concerning the powerful preaching of the gospel. No doubt there are such verses in the Word, but if we have a balanced and proper view when looking into the Word, we can see that the most important thing is the testimony of our life. Is it a miracle for the branches of a vine to bear fruit? Some may refer to the preaching in Acts, but I would refer you to the Gospel of John. Do you believe more in miracles or in life? Do you live more by medicine or by normal food? Medicine is very useful, and many times we need it. However, medicines are only for healing. The bearing of fruit by the branches is the overflow, the outworking of the inner life. We simply abide in the Lord and let Him abide in us, and we deal with all the hindrances to life and fellowship between us and the Lord. In this way we pave the way for the Lord to live Himself out through us. That is the real bearing of fruit.

We may like to take the easy way, the miraculous way. We would like to go to sleep one night and the next morning be full of fruit. That is a dream. Consider the orchards. In any kind of orchard the trees grow, and the husbandman labors. He waters and cares for the plants, and the plants grow. Then gradually, at a certain point, they bear fruit. There is nothing miraculous in an orchard. The church is an orchard. We should not have the dream that all of a sudden we will be full of fruit.

Someone may ask, "What about Pentecost?" Pentecost was the result of the work and labor of the Lord Jesus for three and a half years. It was also the result of one hundred twenty people giving up their country, their family, and their everything. Even at the cost of their lives they stayed in Jerusalem, regardless of the threatening situation, and they prayed for ten days. Have you paid the cost? If you have not paid the price, how can you claim the power of Pentecost? Pentecost was the harvest of the labor of the Lord Jesus for many years. How much have you labored? You cannot have a dream; you have to drop all the dreams. Brothers, let us be normal. We must realize our duty, our responsibility, and our labor. We have to work, we have to pray, we have to spend whatever we have, and we have to be willing to be spent in whatever we are. Take this as a real burden, not as a dream.

### THE GOSPEL BEING A LIFELONG MATTER OF LIVING AND LABORING IN THE LORD

Learn to fellowship with the Lord and to live in, by, and with the Lord. Learn to walk in the presence of the Lord. Then in this way, if we have the desire to cooperate with the Lord, He will open the way. He will pave the way for us to contact our neighbors, schoolmates, classmates, and relatives. It is by this that we will bring people to the Lord; it is by this that we will bear the real fruit. I say again, this is not a work, a movement, or an activity. This is a Christian living, and since it is a living, it must be normal. A living is not miraculous. We must have a living in a normal way. Many times the Lord did some genuine miracles in the church. I have no doubt about this. I saw this kind of thing, but it did not happen most of the time. Most of the time the gospel is normal. We live for Christ, and we walk with Him. We come together, we pray, and we declare and proclaim the Lord's victory. Then the Lord will pave the way and open the door for us to bring people in.

This is a lifelong matter, a matter for the long run. We must change our idea. We cannot have these things as something in a dream. In Matthew 28:19 the Lord spoke concerning the preaching of the gospel, saying, "Disciple all the nations." In addition, the apostle Paul said that when he preached the gospel, he travailed (Gal. 4:19). To travail is to bring forth, to deliver, a child. All mothers know how much they are spent in travail for their children. We have to spend, and we have to be spent. We are not only preaching the gospel; we are living here for the gospel. This is our life, and this is our living.

In order to have long-lived preaching, we have to make this matter normal. Anything that is normal has a long life, but nothing miraculous can have long life. We can never live in a miraculous way. We have to live by the normal way. I do not oppose the miraculous way, but that is neither in my hand nor in your hand. That is in the hand of the Lord. Our duty and our responsibility must be normal. We are here for the preaching of the gospel, so we must have a living for the gospel.

## THE GOSPEL REQUIRING A PRACTICAL, REAL TESTIMONY IN OUR DAILY LIFE

This requires us to be overcomers; it requires a real overcoming life. Our life must be victorious and overcoming. This is especially true in this country. This is not a heathen country. Although there is a good number of unsaved ones, nearly all the people have heard something about the gospel. Therefore, in this country there is an even greater need for a testimony in our daily walk, a testimony in the way we live. We must have a practical, real testimony in our daily life. If someone is a teacher, he must be different from the other teachers. In the office as a co-worker or employee, we have to be different, not in the negative sense but in a very positive sense.

In addition, we have to spend something, and we have to be spent. We cannot do the work of preaching in a light way or in the way of a dream that we will receive special power in order to bring in many people. According to history, a greater percentage of people has been saved through a proper testimony than through the so-called miraculous way. I was not brought to the Lord in a miraculous way. I did see a great number of people brought to the Lord through the miraculous way, but regrettably not many of them still stand fast. It is mostly those who are brought to the Lord through the testimony in the lives of the believers that stand steadfast and grow in life. From my whole Christian life I cannot point out many persons who were saved through miracles that could stand fast and grow adequately. There are some, but very few. However, I can point out many others who stand fast in the Lord and grow adequately. Through what means were they saved? It was through a life testimony. We must all realize that the preaching of the gospel must be a part of our life.

### THE GOSPEL IN OUR DAILY LIVING
### BEING AN ITEM OF THE LORD'S RECOVERY

I believe that among us the Lord will recover mainly four items. First, we must learn to experience Christ in the spirit in a living way. This is the basic matter, the foundation. We must know Christ not in mere teachings nor in the gifts, but in life—the inner life and our daily life in the spirit. Second, we must realize the proper ground of the oneness of the Body. We must always keep the oneness and not do anything in a divisive way. Wherever we go and wherever we are, we keep the unique ground of oneness. In this way we can fulfill God's eternal purpose, coming together to have a local expression of the very Christ whom we experience. Third, whenever we come together on the ground of the local church, we need to have the living, rich, adequate functioning in the meetings to express Christ. In order to express Christ in the church meetings, the saints must exhibit the riches of Christ. Fourth, we must have the outreach of the gospel through our daily living.

These four items—to know Christ as our life, to come together as a local expression to exhibit Christ, to have a rich functioning in our meetings, and to reach out to others to bring them into the Lord's testimony—are the main items in the recovery of the Lord's testimony.

## THE GOSPEL BEING CARRIED OUT IN A NORMAL WAY, NOT MAINLY THROUGH MEETINGS FOR PREACHING

We must realize that the preaching of the gospel is not a kind of movement among us. This is a part of our daily living. Therefore, we all have to live for this and work and labor for this day by day. In order to help us, we sometimes need to have a gospel preaching meeting, but we do not trust very much in the gospel meeting. This is just a small part of our gospel preaching. The main part of gospel preaching is our daily living. Even if we do not have a gospel preaching meeting, after one or two months we still will baptize some new ones. This is normal.

We must not follow the way of today's Christianity to have a campaign and then baptize people. That is not normal. The normal way is that we in this city simply live in, with, and by Christ. We come together to express Christ and serve Christ one to another. Then we have a testimony to the unbelievers, and some of them are brought in. Without any kind of gospel preaching meeting, new converts are baptized into the Body again and again. This is the normal preaching of the church. I do not mean that we never need a gospel preaching meeting, but I stress the normal way because the traditional way of preaching cannot have a long life. We cannot have a healthy, long life by taking medicine. We can live a long and healthy life only by taking normal, proper food. Our preaching can endure only by the normal way.

## A PARTICULAR WORK FOR THE GOSPEL BEING REQUIRED BASED ON OUR LIFE AND TESTIMONY

The proper preaching of the gospel first depends on our testimony. If we brothers and sisters do not have the proper testimony in our daily living, our preaching will be poor. It will never be prevailing because we will not be able to gain the ground with people. If we all live in Christ and have a real testimony in our daily living, we will gain the ground in our neighborhood, office, and school and among our relatives. This testimony paves the way and gains the ground for the gospel. Then once we have the ground through our living testimony in our daily life, we have to work. First we have the life; then we have to work based on the life. In any kind of orchard, there must be life. The growing of the plants is something of life. However, we also need to work, the more the better.

Two brothers may work together with some sisters, coming together to pray, fellowship, and determine what main steps are needed to take care of the new ones. The first step may be to determine whether they have believed in the Lord Jesus with repentance and confession. We should pray for a person specifically with this in view, and after that we can go to contact him. If we find that he has not truly believed, we have to do something to help him to believe. Also, if we find that he did not have a real repentance and confession, we must explain what it means to repent and confess and help him to know how to repent and confess. This requires that we know how to work, just as carpenters learn how to make furniture out of raw materials. Otherwise, we will do things only in a very general way. This is a lifelong business, a business for the long run, and we must all learn how to do it. Second, we may need to know if the new ones are clear about salvation. As a third step we should know if they are ready and willing to be baptized, and then we should know if they are clear about the church life. If we coordinate in this way, we will help each other mutually.

Each step should be carried out within a deadline of one week. Then after three or four weeks of contacting people in this way, we will be clear about their condition. We should be flexible, though; this is simply an illustration with principles. However, we still should be legal about some things. Every day, for example, we have to sleep once and take at least three meals. If we are not a little legal, we cannot have a proper living. Therefore, we are all under the training, and we are learning. We all have to learn not only to preach the gospel but to be built up ourselves. Therefore, we need much coordination. From the past we have learned that to have the adequate coordination, there is the need of certain brothers to bear responsibility to assign something to others. It is by this coordination that the work will go on and on. This requires much exercise and that we be trained through our practice.

To do all this is not too much. This is something we have to work on. Do not forget that, on the one hand, to preach the gospel is to travail, to give new birth to persons. To this end we need to labor. On the other hand, to preach the gospel is to disciple people, to make people disciples of the Lord. To carry out this kind of education requires that we work in a certain way. We trust in the work of the Holy Spirit; there is no doubt about this. However, the principle today is that without human cooperation, even the Holy Spirit cannot do much. The Spirit's work needs and depends on our cooperation. The more cooperation we render to the Spirit, the more work the Spirit will do, and the better cooperation we render to the Spirit, the better work the Spirit will do. We need to render an adequate and better coordination with the Holy Spirit.

Sometimes after contacting someone we may encounter certain problems. There may be some problems that are hard to deal with, and we may be unable to solve them. Then in coordination we may determine which brothers can handle this matter. Some brothers may have experience and be able to help this kind of person. We may even feel that one brother is not adequate, so we can assign two brothers to deal with the problems. It is in this way that the whole "machine" will work. This is the way for many brothers to coordinate. It is the proper way to save time and work efficiently. Whether the "machine" will keep going or will stop, however, depends on how we run it.

## OUR LABOR BEING NOT A HEAVY BURDEN
## BUT OUR NORMAL DUTY

We are limited by time because we are not full-time workers in the gospel. However, if we practice to find the proper way, we can improve our way. I hope we all would learn the best way, not to be too heavily burdened with the work, but to do our work as a duty. We all must learn. We are living here for the gospel. Even if we do not have the time every day, we can separate some time at least once a week for the work of the gospel. If you do a little, I do a little, and every member of the church does a little, we can put all these little portions together into something significant. Moreover, we must do this for the long run, not just once for all or even once a year, but as a regular duty.

If this responsibility is too much for a few brothers, then in fellowship more brothers can be brought in to help. All things can be very flexible. If there are thirty-five new ones, the brothers and sisters can divide into two groups; one can work on seventeen, and the other will work on the other eighteen. The Lord's yoke is not hard, and His burden is not heavy. The Lord has no intention to overwork us. Still, we must look to the Lord for the patience to learn these things.

The proper church life is just like a family life. We cannot build up a family in a miraculous or special way. We have to build up a family in a very normal and ordinary way. This requires our time. It takes at least twenty years for our children to grow up as mature men. The church life is the same way. Even if today we have some miracles in the gospel, I would like to quench them a little. The brothers who were with me in Taiwan can testify that several times after I returned there, I poured cold water on their work if it was done in a miraculous or extraordinary way. This is because I know the danger. If you drive a car eighty miles an hour, I will ask you to slow down a little. It is better to drive thirty or forty miles an hour in a normal way. Recently the son of a co-worker in Taiwan wrote to tell us about the many miracles and healings there. He even laid hands on others, and people were healed. After I read that, I felt to write something to quench his fire a little. I want to help people to take proper food in a normal daily way. Do not eat strange and special foods. Simply eat the normal food; then your family will be healthy.

Dear brothers, I ask you in the Lord's mercy and by His grace to learn a little patience and go on in a proper way. Do not expect too much; simply go on little by little. Then in the long run you will see what the result will be. I have no intention to ask you to overwork. I simply have the desire to see that you all learn how to serve the Lord in a proper, normal way, in the way of life. We are living here for the gospel. As to what we have, we simply spend what we can, and as to what we are, we are willing to be spent for the gospel's sake. Please do your best to work, pray, coordinate, and cooperate. Then this "machine" will keep going on and on. In the long run we will baptize many new ones. This is not too much. Monthly we can have a preaching meeting to help us, and we can all live for the gospel and work in a proper way for the long run. This is a lifelong matter. Gradually, monthly, some new ones will be added into the church. This is just a part of our training. After people are baptized, there is another section of the work that we must care for. Bringing people in is just the beginning, the first part, of gospel preaching.

# CHAPTER TEN

# PREACHING THE GOSPEL
## AS THE ISSUE OF LIFE IN THE CHURCH

Scripture Reading: Phil. 1:5-7, 18-21, 27; John 15:4-5, 8, 12; 17:21; 2:23—3:3

The book of Philippians shows us that the church in Philippi was a church that always bore the gospel as their responsibility. In the New Testament there are a number of Epistles, but only Philippians deals with the preaching of the gospel in such a clear way. We do not have such a clear mention of the gospel in Romans, 1 and 2 Corinthians, Galatians, Ephesians, Colossians, or any of the others. What is mentioned in 1 Timothy is not as clear as what is mentioned in Philippians.

In addition, all Bible students agree that the book of Philippians is a book on the experience of Christ. There is not another book that deals as much with the experience of Christ. If we read this book carefully, we will see that the first chapter tells us Christ is life within us that we may live by Him and live Him out. The second chapter tells us that Christ is the example set up for us. The third chapter tells us that Christ is the mark of the goal, and the fourth chapter tells us that Christ is the secret. Such a short book is very profound and prevailing in the experience of Christ.

## PREACHING THE GOSPEL
### BY THE EXPERIENCE OF CHRIST

Although Philippians is mainly on the experience of Christ, it also deals with the gospel preaching of the church. This shows us that the preaching of the gospel is related to the experience of Christ and is in the experience of Christ. At the beginning of chapter one Paul says that the preaching of the gospel is a good work begun by the Lord and that He will complete this work until the day of Christ Jesus (vv. 5-6). At the end of this chapter, he speaks of striving together—fighting as one, not individually but shoulder to shoulder—along with the faith of the gospel (v. 27). In verses 18 through 21 Paul says, "What then? Only that in every way, whether in pretense or in truthfulness, Christ is announced; and in this I rejoice; yes, and I will rejoice; for I know that for me this will turn out to salvation through your petition and the bountiful supply of the Spirit of Jesus Christ, according to my earnest expectation and hope that in nothing I will be put to shame, but with all boldness, as always, even now Christ will be magnified in my body, whether through life or through death. For to me, to live is Christ and to die is gain." According to the whole context, the proper way to preach the gospel is to live out Christ and magnify Christ in our body. This is not merely to preach by words, and not even to preach by miracles, but to preach by a life which is Christ Himself.

Chapter fifteen of the Gospel of John is on life, while chapter seventeen indicates the building. Verses 4 and 5 of chapter fifteen say, "Abide in Me and I in you. As the branch cannot bear fruit of itself unless it abides in the vine, so neither can you unless you abide in Me. I am the vine; you are the branches. He who abides in Me and I in him, he bears much fruit; for apart from Me you can do nothing." Verse 8 says "In this is My Father glorified, that you bear much fruit and so you will become My disciples," and verse 12 says, "This is My commandment, that you love one another even as I have loved you." In chapter seventeen, verse 21 speaks of the building: "That they all may be one; even as You, Father, are in Me and I in You, that they also may be in Us." Then it speaks of the result, the issue: "That the world may believe that You have sent Me." Chapter fifteen speaks of fruit-bearing through abiding in Christ, and chapter seventeen speaks of the world believing through the oneness of the believers. Our oneness in Christ is the strongest testimony. It is through this that the people in the world realize something of the salvation of

Christ; then they believe that Christ is the very One sent by God.

## PREACHING THE GOSPEL BEING AN ISSUE OF THE INNER LIFE, NOT OF MIRACLES

The proper way for the church to preach the gospel is the way of life and building. We have to abide in Christ, live with Christ, and live out Christ, and we have to be built up together as one in love. Then we will be prevailing in the preaching of the gospel. What then of miracles? This same book shows us where the miracles are in the preaching of the gospel. Verse 23 of chapter two says, "Now when He was in Jerusalem at the Passover, during the feast, many believed into His name when they saw the signs which He did." The miracles seemed to bring many to Christ. Then verses 24 and 25 say, "But Jesus Himself did not entrust Himself to them, for He knew all men, and because He did not need anyone to testify concerning man, for He Himself knew what was in man." The Lord Jesus would not commit Himself to anyone who came in through the miracles. There is no doubt that the miracles brought a crowd to Jesus, but Jesus did not commit Himself to them.

In the original text of the Scriptures there are no chapters and verses. Therefore, chapter three continues chapter two. Chapter three begins, "But there was a man of the Pharisees named Nicodemus, a ruler of the Jews. This one came to Him by night and said to Him, Rabbi, we know that You have come from God as a teacher, for no one can do these signs that You do unless God is with him. Jesus answered and said to him, Truly, truly, I say to you, Unless one is born anew, he cannot see the kingdom of God" (vv. 1-3). It is not a matter of miracles but a matter of being born again. The Lord Jesus would never commit Himself to anyone who came in through the miracles unless that one was born again. In chapter two a crowd of people, stirred up and convinced by miracles, came to Jesus, but Jesus would not commit Himself to them. Then between chapters two and three there is the big word *but*. "But" there was a man who came to Him to have personal contact.

Even Nicodemus had the wrong concept. He saw the signs that Jesus did, so he thought Jesus must be someone great, a great rabbi. However, the Lord Jesus pointed him to the way of life, indicating to him that what he needed was not a teacher but One who gives life, not one who does miracles but One who generates people. It is as if Jesus said, "What you need is not teaching or miracles. What you need is the inner life. You need to be born again."

We must give up our wrong concept from our background and natural understanding. The preaching of the gospel is a part of the church life. We are the members of the Body of Christ. The Body as a whole is the very vessel to contain the Lord and to express Him. The church's preaching, therefore, must be the issue of the church life. If we all live by Christ and with Christ, spontaneously we are the living and functioning branches of the great vine tree. He is the vine tree, and we—the members of His Body—are the branches. When we abide in Him and let Him abide in us, spontaneously the issue is that we bear fruit. The bearing of fruit by the branches is the outworking of the inner life, the manifestation, the expression, of the inner life. When we abide in the vine and let the vine abide in us, the life of the vine nourishes us, saturates us, and bears fruit through us. The outward fruit-bearing is the work of the inner life. It is something spontaneous in life, not something in activity or in the so-called power and miracles. The bearing of fruit by the branches is not something miraculous. It is the daily life of the branches. The branches simply abide in the vine and let the vine abide in them. They do not have any special or extraordinary feelings. They just live in that way. Then the life of the vine moves, works, saturates, nourishes, and brings forth fruit.

## PREACHING THE GOSPEL NOT BY MIRACLES
## BUT BY THE DEATH AND RESURRECTION OF CHRIST

This corresponds with the book of Philippians. In that book we can see that the preaching of the gospel is in the experience of Christ and is the experience of Christ. When the apostle Paul preached the gospel, there were some miracles, but eventually he was brought into the realization that the proper preaching is not a matter of miracles but a matter of life. If the gospel preaching were a matter of miracles, Paul would not have been martyred. However, the Lord would not do anything miraculously to deliver His apostle. He left His apostle in the prison to be martyred without a miracle. The unbelievers might have come to challenge Paul, saying, "Paul, where is your Jesus? If He is able, He should save you. It seems that He is not as powerful as we are. We put you into prison, and He can do nothing to save you."

Even the Lord Jesus Himself suffered this kind of challenge, yet He would not do anything to save Himself. Let us learn the lesson. The more that people say that we are poor, the more we have to be poor. Any kind of challenge is from the enemy, and we should never take it. The people said, "If You are the Son of God, come down from the cross!" (Matt. 27:40). It is as if the Lord replied, "No. For you there is no other sign but the sign of the prophet Jonah. I have to die, and I have to be buried." Never be challenged. The Lord Jesus, who was God, was never successfully challenged. The more people challenged Him, the more He was silent. Today the gospel is prevailing through death and resurrection. The Lord did no miracle to deliver the apostle from prison, but there was the mighty, prevailing manifestation of Christ through this apostle. He said, "Christ will be magnified in my body, whether through life or through death. For to me, to live is Christ" (Phil. 1:20b-21a). This is the real preaching of the gospel.

## NOT HAVING A MOVEMENT BUT ABIDING IN CHRIST AND BEING BUILT UP TOGETHER

I look to the Lord that we all would not expect anything in a miraculous way. Rather, we all must pray, fellowship with the Lord, and learn to abide in Christ, to be built up, and to be one in Christ. Then we will allow life to flow out to generate others, to bring life to others. This kind of preaching will be a part of our life, a part of our living, and a part of the church life. We all must realize that we do not have a certain kind of activity. We do not encourage the brothers to have a movement. This is not a movement. If we consider this as a movement, we are one hundred percent wrong; we are "in one bed with different dreams." I speak the truth: I do not have the dream that we are here in a movement or activity. I say one hundred times "no." I have the clear vision that we are here simply as small Christians. We are poor and we are nothing. We have nothing and we do not want to have anything. We never pretend to be anything, but by the Lord's mercy, we want to learn how to live and abide in Him and how to be built up with one another.

I am just a little finger; by myself I am nothing. We as members have to be built up together as a living Body—living by Christ, living with Christ, and living out Christ. This is the proper Christian life. If you would receive the mercy and grace of the Lord, forget about your background. I was in a certain background for years, but I have forgotten it. We must never be so foolish as to neglect the lessons of history throughout the last two thousand years. The proper way to bring people to Christ is the way of life, and the proper way for the church to be built up is also the way of life. We are not the people in the first century. We are in the twentieth century. Nineteen centuries have passed already, and there have been many lessons.

Many persons sought the miraculous things, but what came out of that? I would ask someone to point out from history the benefit of that. On the day of Pentecost there were miracles, but what was there after that? Was there the real building up of the church in the book of Acts? It seems only that jealousy and other problems came in. There was not the real building up. After Acts there is the book of Romans. Is there anything miraculous mentioned in the book of Romans? After that we need the two Epistles to the Corinthians to adjust us from the wrong thought to the life of the cross. Then there is Ephesians, the unique book written purposely concerning the church. Is there anything miraculous in the book of Ephesians? Let us come to the Lord in a quiet way, forgetting about our backgrounds. The proper way to have the church life today is the way of life, to know Christ inwardly, to know our flesh, our self, and the natural man through the cross, and to learn to abide in Christ and live by Christ, not by ourselves. Then we will be built up together. Then we will have a spontaneous issue of the church life, which will be the prevailing and proper preaching.

We must be delivered from the wrong concept. Never be frustrated; do not challenge yourself and do not be challenged by others to try to have the power to do miracles. Forget about that. I saw much of that in the past. Recently in Taiwan six hundred people were healed in two days. To speak the truth, however, I do not appreciate that very much. We all have to learn to know Christ in the living way, in the inner way, to know Christ in our spirit. It is in Christ as our inner life that we are built up as one to be a living expression, the living Body to express Him. And it is through this expression that people gradually, one after another, are brought into the life of Christ and also into the church life. It is in this way that the gospel will be preached and the Body will be built up.

Never be frustrated, never be confused, never challenge yourself, and never be challenged by others. I say boldly that the way of miraculous preaching is the wrong way. The right way for the church to be built up is the way of life, and the right way for the church to preach the gospel is also the way of life. Do not listen to so many voices. Within you there is the discernment. The Lord Jesus said that His sheep hear His voice (John 10:16). Do you feel those challenges are the voice of the Lord Jesus? There is no need to argue. We must use our inward discernment to realize what voice is the voice of the Shepherd.

I would like to stress a thousandfold: The proper way for the church to be built up is the way of life. We do not want to have any more confusion. There already has been too much confusion and frustration in history, even up until today. We do not like to have these frustrations again. We want to be simple. We just pay attention to one thing, that is, Christ as our life and everything. We do not care for anything else. Do not be frustrated and confused, and do not frustrate and confuse others. Simply learn to be simple. We are nothing. We are just little members of Christ. Therefore, we must learn to live in Him, live with Him, and be built up together. We do not expect and we do not appreciate those miraculous things. This is my speaking not only today; since I have been in this country it has been the same. The trouble I have seen in various places was simply that people repeated the tragedy of history. We, however, have learned the lessons from history, and we do not like to repeat the tragedies.

Forget about teachings, the so-called gifts, miracles, and other such matters. Only one thing works well, that is, to take Christ as life in an inner way and to be built up in this life as the living Body. All the apostles—Peter, Paul, and John—were brought into this same realization when they became old. Read their writings. In the last book of the whole Scriptures, Revelation, nothing miraculous is presented in a positive way. According to Revelation 13, it is the Antichrist and his false prophet that will do many miraculous things when they rise up. Rather, Revelation tells us clearly that we have to sacrifice, to die, to be martyred, as the last apostle, the aged John, did.

Learn to live by Christ, live with Christ, and live in Christ, and learn to be built up in this life. Then the preaching of the gospel will be the issue of this kind of life. I look to the Lord that we all will be brought into such a proper understanding. Allow me to say once again, we have to forget about our backgrounds. We must not be influenced by the backgrounds. We are not speaking here about preaching in the old way of our old backgrounds. We are talking about gospel preaching as a part of the church life. I look to the Lord, and I hope that one day the church here will have not only a formal gospel preaching, but that gradually people will be brought into the church not mainly through that kind of preaching but through the daily living of the believers. Do not have the concept from your old background that we are having a kind of movement or activity. Rather, when we speak about the preaching of the gospel, we mean that it is a part of the church life. This is why in this message we have read from Philippians and the Gospel of John, to show us that the preaching of the gospel is a part of the church life.

I say again, do not challenge yourself, do not challenge others, and do not be challenged to take the way of movement or miracles. We simply realize that we are little members of Christ, abiding in Him, learning to live with Him and to be built up together. Then we believe there will be the spontaneous issue that people will be brought into the church life through us. This is the genuine gospel preaching.

## COORDINATING AND BEING BLENT TOGETHER TO CARE FOR PEOPLE

In the past we learned that preaching the gospel in the church is a very good means for us to be brought together, to be fitly framed and mingled one with another. Therefore, there is the real need for some brothers and sisters to bear the responsibility for the mingling. They have to be the "blenders." If we coordinate well in the gospel, all the brothers and sisters will be blended together. We are too independent, and we like too much to be private. To be Christians, however, we cannot always keep our privacy. We have to be blended with others. If we are all blended, this will give a very strong impression to the unbelievers and new converts.

A brother may pray for a friend, a relative, a neighbor, or a classmate, preach the gospel to him, and have a certain amount of contact with him. Even in material matters, though, it is not prevailing for someone to do something by himself. It is more prevailing for him to ask one, two, or even five brothers to help him to deal with this person. If in the church there are certain ones who bear some responsibility, the brother can submit the name of his friend or relative to them with particular details. Then these responsible ones can consider this person, and they may realize what his need is. They may realize that this person needs a certain other brother to help take care of him, and they can pass this name on to that brother. Then that brother should take this as a responsibility from the Lord. Spontaneously he will contact the first brother to fellowship about the new one, and then they will find out what they must do. Then after one or two weeks the responsible ones may look into the situation again and feel that this person can be cared for further by a third brother, and they will pass the burden to him. This is simply an illustration of the principle of blending.

If we take this way, our friends and neighbors will realize that Christians are wonderful people—old and young, high and low, American and Chinese, all working together as one for one goal. This will be a strong testimony to them, and it will be very easy to bring them to the Lord. Then after they are saved, it will be easy to bring them into the church life. From this we can foresee and anticipate that the building of the Body will be realized through this kind of preaching.

The whole church, all the members, must be prevailing to function in preaching the gospel. This is the main part of the church life. The church lives here for the testimony of Jesus, to win people from the usurping hand of the enemy. We are living here day by day for this, and we fight for this. To live for the gospel is the proper way to have the church life. Monthly and yearly, we live for the gospel to win people for Christ. We are not seeking merely to be spiritual. Rather, we are living for Christ to expand and enlarge His kingdom.

We must realize the proper way to carry out the gospel preaching, and we must realize that our purpose as the living Body is to defeat the enemy and to release, to win, the souls who are under his usurping hand. This is carried out simply by the living of the church, by the church life. We do expect that one day the church here would not have any outward preaching meetings, yet each month a certain number of people will still be brought into the church. This is the normal way. A good number of people will be able to stand up to give testimonies telling how they were saved simply through the living testimony of the dear brothers and sisters. We all must agree to learn this way, to abide in the Lord, to live with Him, and to be built up together.

We should submit the names of those we contact to others for fellowship. These persons will then become the material with which we work. When we receive the names of people to care for, we should never do it by ourselves. We should do things in a cooperating way, contacting related brothers or sisters to pray and fellowship with them. It is in this way that we all will be built up together more and more. We will have much fellowship in this matter. How wonderful that will be! This is the flow of the lifeblood in the Body; if we have this flow, the Body will be healthy.

## HELPING PEOPLE TO EXPERIENCE
## THE LORD'S SALVATION
## THROUGH REPENTANCE AND FORGIVENESS OF SINS

*Question:* A man of about eighty years old came to our gospel meeting. Coming from a religious background, he likes to visit with us, but he seems satisfied merely to be saved. How should we go on with a person like this?

*Answer:* With such an aged person, we first must find out whether or not he has been truly saved. Then if he has been saved, we have to find out whether or not he has the assurance of being saved. If we have some doubt about these two matters, we should endeavor to help this person to realize the Lord's salvation. However, if he has been saved and has the assurance of salvation, we have to praise and thank the Lord. Then if we have more time, and if we have only this one person in our hands, we can help him further and work on him for the Lord. However, if we do not have much time, if we have more persons to take care of, there may be no need to spend more time with him.

*Question:* A few months ago a certain person came to the United States from Taiwan and is now learning English. He senses the emptiness of this world and was touched by the gospel. He prayed with us, but he needs more help in the confirmation of salvation. He is very busy now. How should we follow up on him?

*Answer:* This person needs some real help to pray with repentance, to confess his sins. All the brothers who have contacted him need to pray for him, to remember him before the Lord that the Lord would grant him the repentance and forgiveness of sins. Acts 5:31 speaks of repentance and forgiveness of sins. This indicates that at a certain point this kind of person must not only realize that he needs Christ and must not only believe in Christ, but he must repent before the Lord. We cannot cause people to repent. This requires a work of the mercy of God. More or less, we have passed on the knowledge of the gospel to him, but now we have to pray for him, because there is the need of the real work of the Holy Spirit within him to cause him to repent. Then he will confess his sins and experience the forgiveness of sins. At that time his spirit will be made alive. First, all the brothers who have contacted him need to pray for him. Then the next brother who contacts him needs to help him to realize a real repentance and a living confession. This will require some fellowship with him, some kind of talk to help him to realize his need. Then the Holy Spirit will have the ground to make his spirit alive. No doubt he is busy, but when his spirit is made alive, something will energize him from within, and he will spare some time for coming to the meetings. If we do not do this, we will merely help him to be religious; that does not help much.

### TAKING THE PROPER WAY TO PREACH THE GOSPEL THROUGH THE CHURCH

If we take the way we have fellowshipped here, the Holy Spirit will work wonderful things. What we do will pave the way and open the door for the Holy Spirit to come in, not only to work on the unbelievers but also to work on us. It is in this way that "one stone will kill two birds"—we will have both the gospel preaching and the building up of the church. This will cause us all to be living. We will spend our life, our time, our energy, and our money for the Lord's kingdom, winning souls for the Lord. This will be very much blessed by the Lord, and it will influence people.

If we love one another and cooperate in coordination, this will influence the people of the world. If we are one in Christ, the world will believe that the Lord Jesus is the Christ, the One sent by God. This will be a real influence on the unbelievers. In this way the doors will gradually open widely and effectively. Therefore, we have to build this up. If we go on in this way, we will see a glorious outcome. We can compare this to an orchard. If we work on it a little to plant and care for it, one day we will have glorious blossoms and bountiful fruit. We are working here to build up an orchard. Many trees will grow up and will bear fruit. This is the proper way for the preaching of the gospel through the church.

We are now on the right course. The only thing we need now is for all the brothers and sisters to continue to work some more. I hope that we all will work by prayer. We should pray for all the names that come to us, remembering them before the Lord. It is not by us that people are saved; it is by the Lord Himself. We simply pave the way; we open the door. We are the channel, the influence, but the living One must be the Lord Himself. He is the only living One, so He must come in. Therefore, we have to pray whenever we receive the names of new contacts, and we should pass their names on to others for them to pray also. I believe that the Lord will honor this kind of prayer. We work through prayer. We do not have any trust in ourselves, in our doing, or in our working. We trust in the Lord Himself, and we simply do our duty to cooperate with Him.

I look to the Lord and pray that we all will learn to go on in this way, in the way of life and in the way of being built up. Then the Lord will be lived out through us and be ministered to others, and they will receive life. More materials will be added to the church, and the church will be built up in a living way. Brothers and sisters, go on in this way. We will see the glorious result in the long run.

# CHAPTER ELEVEN

# BEING A LIVING TESTIMONY
# FOR THE INCREASE OF CHRIST

Scripture Reading: John 3:25-30; 12:20-26, 32-33; 15:1-5, 7-8, 12, 16-17; 17:21-23

We all must cooperate to carry out the burden of these messages in prayer. This is not only a burden but a battle. We have to realize that in all the priestly service there is always a battle. We are not dealing merely with a work; we are dealing with an evil force in the heavenlies, the force of darkness. How much we need the prevailing prayers! Please join in the spirit to pray for this training. Through all my recent visits to other places, I realize that there is a real, urgent, and desperate need for this kind of training. We pray that the Lord would work out these matters among us, in us, and through us.

## THE GENUINE GOSPEL REVEALED IN JOHN

Many Christians do not have the thought that the Gospel of John deals with the real outreach of gospel preaching. However, the best and proper way for the outreach of the gospel is clearly revealed in this book. John was written not only with a particular sequence, or order, but with a process, from the very beginning through to the ultimate consummation. In this Gospel there are twenty-one chapters, which are divided into three sections. The first section, mostly from chapter one to chapter three, shows us the birth of life. For instance, 1:12 says, "But as many as received Him, to them He gave the authority to become children of God, to those who believe into His name." Then 3:6 tells us that this birth is a birth in the spirit and of the Spirit: "That which is born of the Spirit is spirit."

Then the second section, from chapter four through at least chapter seven, deals with the growth of life. After a baby is born, he needs to grow by eating and drinking. Chapter four makes it very clear that we have to drink of Christ as the living fountain (vv. 10, 14). To drink is different from being born. To drink is to grow after being born. Then in chapter six Jesus tells us that we have to eat Him: "He who eats Me, he also shall live because of Me" (v. 57b). We have to feed on Him. To feed is not only to receive Christ but to take Him as our life supply. Life is for birth, while life supply is for the growth of life. After birth we have the growth of life.

The third section is mostly from chapter ten or eleven to the end of the book. To say that the point of this section is maturity in life does not express it adequately. Of course, from birth we receive life, by eating and drinking we grow, and by growing we attain the fullness of life, that is, maturity. However, maturity is for building. Near the close of this book there is the prayer of the Lord in chapter seventeen: "That they all may be one; even as You, Father, are in Me and I in You, that they also may be in Us; that the world may believe that You have sent Me" (v. 21). This oneness is the building. The third section of this book, therefore, is the building.

Many Christians take it for granted that this Gospel is a book for beginners. However, this book includes eternity past and eternity future. Eternity past is indicated in 1:1, which says, "In the beginning was the Word, and the Word was with God, and the Word was God." Then in eternity future there is a building. As we have seen many times, this building is a mutual habitation of God and man, and it is the universal, great vine tree. In chapter fifteen there is the vine tree with all the branches. The vine itself is the Head, and all the branches are the members of the Body. If we look only at the branches, it seems that they are separate, but if we trace them to the source, we can see that they are all built together in the vine as one. This oneness is the building. In chapter two the Lord said that His physical body was a temple on a small scale. He predicted that the enemy would utilize the

Jewish people to destroy this body: "Destroy this temple, and in three days I will raise it up" (v. 19). This refers to the resurrection. By resurrection and in resurrection Christ built up a universal building in oneness.

## THE BRIDE OF CHRIST
## BEING THE INCREASE OF CHRIST

John 3:25 through 30 say, "There arose therefore a questioning on the part of John's disciples with a Jew about purification. And they came to John and said to him, Rabbi, He who was with you across the Jordan, of whom you have testified, behold, He is baptizing and all are coming to Him. John answered and said, A man cannot receive anything unless it has been given to him from heaven. You yourselves testify of me that I said, I am not the Christ, but I have been sent before Him. He who has the bride is the bridegroom; but the friend of the bridegroom, who stands and hears him, rejoices with joy because of the bridegroom's voice. This joy of mine therefore is made full. He must increase, but I must decrease."

We have to join verse 29 to verse 30. In verse 29 there is the bride, and in verse 30 there is the increase. This shows us that the bride is the increase of Christ, just as Eve, the wife of Adam, was the increase of Adam. Originally Adam was single, a bachelor, but later an increase came out of him. That increase was the increase of Adam himself, who became his counterpart, a bride. Even in type it is very clear that the bride, or the wife, is always an increase of the bridegroom, the husband. In John 3, John the Baptist says that the increase of Christ is His very bride.

### THE WAY TO HAVE THE INCREASE OF CHRIST

In chapter three, however, we cannot see the way to have the increase of Christ. The way is revealed in chapter twelve. John 12:20 to 23 say, "And there were some Greeks among those who went up to worship at the feast. These then came to Philip, who was from Bethsaida of Galilee, and asked him, saying, Sir, we wish to see Jesus. Philip came and told Andrew; Andrew came, and Philip too, and they told Jesus.

And Jesus answered them, saying, The hour has come for the Son of Man to be glorified." If we stop here, we may think that to be glorified is to be put on the throne. We have to realize the situation. All the people at this time welcomed Jesus. They rendered the biggest, warmest welcome to Him. Even the Gentiles, the Greeks, came to greet Him and the disciples, such as Philip, Andrew, and the others. I believe that they must have been excited. If you and I had been there, we would have been excited. This was something that never had happened in those three and a half years. However, while the disciples were excited and came to tell it to the Lord, He said "The hour has come for the Son of Man to be glorified."

Verse 24 says, "Truly, truly, I say to you, Unless the grain of wheat falls into the ground and dies, it abides alone; but if it dies, it bears much fruit." *Fruit* here refers to the many grains. To be glorified is to undergo the process of death and resurrection. Verses 25 and 26 continue, "He who loves his soul-life loses it; and he who hates his soul-life in this world shall keep it unto eternal life. If anyone serves Me, let him follow Me; and where I am, there also My servant will be. If anyone serves Me, the Father will honor him." Then verses 32 and 33 say, "And I, if I be lifted up from the earth, will draw all men to Myself. But He said this signifying by what kind of death He was about to die." Do not think that to be lifted up is to be enthroned. Rather, this lifting up was His being put to death. John 12 reveals the way of increase. The increase of Christ is brought forth and produced by the process of death and resurrection.

## THE PREACHING OF THE GOSPEL
## BEING FOR THE INCREASE OF CHRIST

In these portions of the Word there is the real preaching and outreach of the gospel. First, we must point out that the real meaning of the outreach of the gospel is the increase of Christ. The preaching, the furtherance, of the gospel is the increase of Christ. The real preaching causes Christ to be increased. This is not merely my thought or concept. This is the thought even of John the Baptist. The disciples of John were with John and for John. They wanted to see people following John, but they saw something different, that is, that people came to Jesus instead of John. Therefore they became jealous, and one day they came to John and said, "Rabbi,...He is baptizing and all are coming to Him" (3:26). Their tone was one of jealousy. Then John seemed to answer, "I told you clearly from the first day that I am not the Christ. I am just a voice for Christ. He is the Christ, and He is the One who will have the bride."

Whether or not those poor disciples understood John's word, we have to understand it. All the people who came to Christ and received something of Him eventually became the bride of Christ. The bride is the composition of all the people who receive Christ. Therefore, John could say, "Do not be jealous. I am the baptizer, not the bridegroom. He is the Bridegroom. It is right for all the people to go to Him, because He is the One who will have the bride." Then John said, "He must increase, but I must decrease." When we read these two words together, *bride* and *increase*, we spontaneously can understand that the bride is the increase, and the increase is the bride.

To preach the gospel is to bring people to Christ. Regrettably, however, many Christians today do not realize that to bring people to Christ is to have Christ increased. In our gospel preaching have we ever had the thought that we are bringing people to be part of the bride of Christ, that we are bringing people for the increase of Christ? For more than twenty years I did not have the thought that gospel preaching is a matter of Christ being increased and of more people being added to the bride of Christ. In John 3 the gospel is for the increase of Christ. This is not the gospel of going to heaven. Many in Christianity have the thought that because people are pitiful and will go to hell after they die, they must realize that God loves them and sent His Son to save them and bring them to heaven. However, we should listen to the first evangelist, John the Baptist. In the Bible there is the principle of the first mention; the first time anything is mentioned, that sets the principle for that thing. The first evangelist told us that to bring people to Christ is to increase Christ and constitute the bride of Christ.

The more I remained with the Lord considering these messages, the more I felt from the Lord that the dear brothers and sisters must be helped to realize that the real gospel preaching is the increase of Christ, and the real outreach of the gospel that brings people to Christ is to compose the bride of Christ. From now on when we are going out to preach the gospel, we have to change our attitude. We have to have our concept transformed. The gospel is not merely to save the fallen sinners; it is to have Christ increased. It is to bring in more of the parts of the bride of Christ. This is very basic, because if we do not realize what the true meaning of gospel preaching is, we will take the wrong way in our preaching.

### GENUINE PREACHING BEING
### A LIFE OF CRUCIFIXION AND RESURRECTION
### TO MANIFEST CHRIST

As we have said, John 12 shows us the way for Christ to be increased. How can one grain of wheat be increased into many grains? We often speak of verse 24, but most of the time we think that this verse applies only to Christ as the one grain. We must realize that in principle this verse is also for us. In these days, we at least have a heart to preach the gospel. Do we realize that to preach the gospel is to have Christ increased through us? We are one grain. How then can this one grain be multiplied? It is not merely by telling our neighbor, "You have to realize that you are a sinner. God loves you, and I love you too. You need Christ." There is nothing wrong with this, but it is too short.

We preach the gospel not only by speaking. While we speak with our neighbor, the enemy Satan, the subtle one, may work within him, causing him to think, "You say I have not been saved. Do you mean that you are saved? What is the difference between you and me? Are you better than I? If I am a poor sinner, how about you? To me, you are more poor." The subtle one puts many questions within that person, so this kind of preaching may not work. We cannot convince such a person, and he can point his finger and ask, "What about you and your mother, your wife, your brother, and all your in-laws? You have too many problems. Let me tell you how to deal with your wife. I do not need your preaching; you need my preaching." Sometimes our relatives, neighbors, school-mates, and colleagues are polite. They would not say a word outwardly, but they say much within themselves. Sometimes, even many times, the more we preach, the more nothing happens, and people become disgusted with our preaching. In this case it may be better to be silent.

How can the one grain be increased into many grains today? It is by a real crucified life, by being a crucified person, dying day by day. Here is the universal principle. Where there is the divine death, there is the divine resurrection. If we simply will die, Christ will be resurrected. It is by this process of death and resurrection that Christ is manifested to our friends and neighbors. There may be no need for us to preach very much. If we are lifted up on the cross, this will attract people to Christ.

We need a real testimony by experiencing the death and resurrection of Christ in our daily life. If we do not have a real testimony in life, then the more we preach, the more we will hinder the gospel. Many dear Christians simply cannot preach the gospel to their relatives because they have no testimony. No one knows our lives better than our relatives. If we cannot have a proper testimony in life through death and resur-rection, then the more we live in a place, the more all the neighbors will keep away from us. The real preaching is a life of crucifixion and resurrection to manifest Christ. This convinces people. Do not argue with people. The more we argue, the more we lose the ground. Rather, we must convince people by our dying, our daily walk, and our daily living.

Throughout the last two thousand years the crucifixion, the death, and the cross of Christ have been speaking to many hearts. We need the death of Christ, we need the cross, and we need the crucifixion to speak Christ more than we need our mouths to speak. This does not mean that we do not need to open our mouth to say something for the Lord. We need this. However, the most basic thing is the life testimony. We need to die; there is no other way. Do not argue with your neighbors, your schoolmates, or your classmates; rather, die to them. Unless a grain of wheat falls into the earth and dies, it can never be multiplied. This multiplication is the very out-reach of the gospel.

We Christians are always dreaming. There is no need to seek the miraculous gift of dreams. We are all experts in dreams. We think that if we pray three nights and three days, we will be empowered, powerful to preach the gospel. In actuality, there is no such thing; I say a thousand times, no. Rather, unless a grain of wheat falls into the earth and dies, there is no multiplication. Regardless of how many days, nights, months, or even years we pray, the answer to proper prayer is, "You have to die." If you are going to have the multi-plication, if you are going to have the increase, you have to die. Unless the grain dies, there is no possibility of any kind of increase.

I say again, this does not mean that we do not need preach-ing by speaking. We need it, but the preaching by speaking must be based on the crucified life. The crucified life must open the way for our speaking. Otherwise, our life will only close the way. Regardless of how much we speak from our mouth, our speaking will only make it worse. If we do not have the life testimony, it is better to shut our mouth. The way of increase is death and resurrection. There is no other way. It seems that John 12:24 applies only to the Lord. If we read on, however, we come to verses 25 and 26, which clearly tell us that the principle of verse 24 is also for us. If we are going to serve the Lord, we have to be in the place where He is. He is in the way of death; He is on the way of the cross. Therefore, we have to be there too.

We all have to see that the real gospel preaching is for the increase of Christ. Christ is in us, so we are a grain. Within us there is life, but there is also the outer shell. This shell has to be broken. It must be put into the earth to die there. Then the inner life, that is Christ Himself, will be manifested, and by this manifestation, Christ will be imparted into others. This imparting is His very increase. It is not simply a matter of preaching the doctrine of the gospel. It is a matter of imparting Christ into others by a life that is crucified and resurrected.

## THE COMMISSION OF THE GOSPEL
## BEING TO REPRODUCE CHRIST FOR HIS INCREASE

John 15 shows us how the many grains are built up together as a corporate increase. In chapter twelve we see the way to produce the increase, and in chapter fifteen we see the way of building. Verses 1 through 5 say, "I am the true vine, and My Father is the husbandman. Every branch in Me that does not bear fruit, He takes it away; and every branch that bears fruit, He prunes it that it may bear more fruit. You are already clean because of the word which I have spoken to you. Abide in Me and I in you. As the branch cannot bear fruit of itself unless it abides in the vine, so neither can you unless you abide in Me. I am the vine; you are the branches. He who abides in Me and I in him, he bears much fruit; for apart from Me you can do nothing."

We may have the wrong concept that the fruit spoken of by the Lord refers to certain manifestations of life, such as the fruit of the Spirit mentioned in Galatians 5. In these days, however, the more I consider this chapter, the more I am becoming clear. John 15:16 shows us the real meaning of fruit in this chapter. This verse says, "You did not choose Me, but I chose you, and I set you that you should go forth and bear fruit and that your fruit should remain, that whatever you ask the Father in My name, He may give you." If we read this verse carefully, we can realize that fruit does not refer to the manifestations of life. To bring forth fruit is to produce, to have an increase. This refers to the genuine outreach of the gospel. It is to impart Christ into people, causing them to become the fruit. In this chapter, fruit is the outflow of Christ into people, thus making them the increase of Christ.

Consider a fruit tree. The fruit on the branches of the tree are the increase of the tree. Fruit is not merely meekness, humility, or a kind of good behavior. It is the overflow of the inner life to produce an increase of life. Fruit trees are reproduced by the seed of the fruit. Within all the fruit on the branches of the tree there are seeds. When these seeds fall into the earth, they produce more trees. Originally there was only one tree, but after a certain time, there are many trees. This is the increase.

At the end of Matthew the Lord gave us the commission to go to the nations to preach the gospel (28:19). In Mark there is a similar word: "Go into all the world and proclaim the gospel to all the creation" (16:15). Likewise, Luke ends in the same way (24:47-49). In the Gospel of John, however, does the Lord's speak there concerning the preaching of the gospel? It is there, but in a different way. In Matthew, Mark, and Luke, it seems that the preaching of the gospel is a movement, a certain kind of activity or work. It is only in the Gospel of John, the Gospel of life, that the preaching of the gospel is not a work or activity; it is an outflow of life. That is why in John 15:16 the Lord chose and set the disciples to go forth and bear fruit. This is to preach the gospel for the increase of Christ. We must go forth to produce Christ, to have Christ reproduced, multiplied, and increased thirtyfold, sixtyfold, or a hundredfold. This is the "great commission." In this book it seems that there is no such commission for gospel preaching, but in actuality there is the real commission of gospel preaching. It is not in a way of work, activity, or movement, but it is in the way of life, in a way of the outflow of the inner life.

### BEING PRUNED IN ORDER TO BEAR MORE FRUIT

According to John 15, if we mean business with the Lord, the Father will prune, cut, and purge us. All the branches need a certain kind of trimming. I am somewhat reluctant to say this because I do not want to disappoint you or scare you away. However, if you go to the best husbandman to ask him how he helps the branches to bear fruit, he will tell you that he prunes them. Some branches do not bear fruit because they are short of pruning. When the brothers and sisters mean business with the Lord, and the Father comes in to put His hand upon them and prune them, right away the preaching of the gospel becomes prevailing. On the other hand, we may be very comfortable. If someone asks, "How are you?", we may say, "Everything is fine." However, everything is not fine for the gospel preaching. The more everything is fine, the more we are not prevailing in gospel preaching. When one day the environment, our situation, is not so fine, even upside down, that will be the prevailing time for gospel preaching.

Many dear saints cannot preach the gospel prevailingly when they are healthy. However, once the Father, the Husbandman, touches the branch a little, their health is gone; they have some kind of illness. At that time their preaching becomes prevailing. While we are prosperous, we may tell people that they need Jesus and that they must believe in Him, but this may be like the daughters of Lot talking to the people in Sodom. People will not care for this kind of speaking and will listen to it in the same way that they listen to the news. However, we may lose our business, lose other things, or have other troubles. We may suffer something. This is the trimming, the cutting, the purging, and the breaking. This will cause us as branches to bring forth fruit. The Husbandman, who is the Father, knows how to prune us.

John 15 is very significant. In this chapter the Father has the intention to work all that He is, all the fullness of the Godhead in Christ, into the branches of the vine that they may bear fruit. There is much need for the Father to work all His fullness into us that we may bear fruit, that is, that we may have the outflow of the inner life, which is the reality of the fullness of the Father. The outflow of the inner life is the fruit, and many times this outflow comes out only by trimming, cutting, and pruning.

### ABIDING IN CHRIST IN ORDER TO BEAR FRUIT

In order to have a prevailing outreach of the gospel, we must learn how to abide in Christ. To abide in Christ means to keep ourselves in fellowship with Christ. All the time we must let Christ abide in us. There must be an inner flow between us and Christ. We have to abide in Him and let Him abide in us. Then whatever He wishes, whatever He speaks, His Word, His intention, will abide within us. There is the need of such a living fellowship between us and the Lord.

Again, this does not mean that we should not open our mouth to preach the gospel. It means that our preaching with our mouth depends on the real inner flow of Christ. We must have the inner flowing in Christ and with Christ. Then, whenever we open our mouth, there will be the prevailing power, not merely an outward power but the power of the inner life.

## ASKING WHATEVER WE WILL FOR FRUIT-BEARING

We also have to learn how to pray for this outreach. John 15:7 and 8 say, "If you abide in Me and My words abide in you, ask whatever you will, and it shall be done for you. In this is My Father glorified, that you bear much fruit and so you will become My disciples." This portion deals with prayer. Whatever we ask, the Father will answer. This means that we ask for certain persons to be brought to the Lord to be a part of the increase of Christ. In the past some young ones came to me and said, "In John 15:7 the Lord promised that whatever we ask, He will give to us. For several years I asked the Lord to give me the best college so I may get a Ph.D., but He has not fulfilled His promise." If we read the context of this chapter, however, we will realize that the prayer mentioned here by the Lord is that certain persons may be brought into the increase of Christ. It is a prayer for people to become fruit as the outflow of the inner life.

If we add all the foregoing items together, we can see where our shortage is and why our preaching is not prevailing. Many in today's Christianity think that gospel preaching is a matter of activities, evangelistic campaigns, and crusades. It is not so. The real gospel preaching is the outflow of Christ through you and through me. That is the increase of Christ.

## BEING BUILT UP IN LOVE
## AS A TESTIMONY TO THE WORLD

John 15:12 says, "This is My commandment, that you love one another even as I have loved you," and verse 17 says, "These things I command you that you may love one another." To love one another here means to be built up. Then chapter seventeen continues in the same way. Verses 21 through 23 say, "That they all may be one; even as You, Father, are in Me and I in You, that they also may be in Us; that the world may believe that You have sent Me. And the glory which You have given Me I have given to them, that they may be one, even as

We are one; I in them, and You in Me, that they may be per-
fected into one, that the world may know that You have sent
Me and have loved them even as You have loved Me." When
we come to chapter seventeen, we all have to humble ourselves. We are all short in this matter. We have not been built
up.

Many Christians today at best have a meeting, but they do
not have the building. They have a piling up of stones, not
a building up. Today I may feel to "pile up" with one dear
brother, but after another two months I may find that he is
not so good, so I shift over to another pile. Do not think that
someone has come to me and told me about your condition. If
anyone has come to me, that must be the Holy Spirit. He has
come to me many times with a rebuke, saying, "Look at the
situation among you." I do not know the details of your story,
but in my spirit I know the principle. Among us there has
been too much "shifting of the piles." Once we are built up,
however, we can never shift. A piece of wood in the building
cannot be shifted; it is simply built up.

Give up the expectation to be shifted. I am built up with
a certain brother, so I love him. I do not love him because he
is loveable. I simply love without a reason. I have to. There is
the imperative that we love one another. When we love one
another, that means that we are truly built up. By this oneness and building up, the world will be convinced.

How can we expect our friends, family, and relatives to be
brought to Christ? Many times our family hears us criticizing
the brothers. When we criticize the church and the dear
brothers and sisters, our children and wife listen to us. After
that, how can we expect them to be brought to the Lord?
Rather, they will just shake their heads at the gospel. On the
contrary, we must love one another. Even if a wife complains
and asks, "How can you love that kind of people?", her husband
can say, "I just love them." That wife's mouth will complain
and criticize, but she will be convinced in her heart.

The best test is the test of the building. How much we have
been dealt with by the Lord and how much we have learned
the lessons must be tested by the building. This is why
in John 15 as the Lord was dealing with fruit-bearing, He

commanded us to love one another. Loving one another has very much to do with the bearing of fruit. If we do not love our brothers and sisters, I do not believe that we can be prevailing in our gospel preaching. If today we criticize a sister, and tomorrow we are unhappy with a brother, and then we preach the gospel, do you think our preaching can be prevailing? The spiritual world is watching. The evil spirits may even speak within us, "Are you preaching the gospel?" There is no convincing power in this kind of preaching. Suppose, however, that we simply love a brother or a sister regardless of what kind of person he or she is. We simply love him without a reason or an explanation. If this is the case, we can be assured that whenever we open our mouth to preach the gospel, there will be the convincing power. The power is not in our voice or loud proclamation. The power is in our convincing life.

If we are going to have a prevailing preaching, we must be pruned by the Father, abide in the Son, pray for people to be brought into the reality of the increase of Christ, love one another, be built up together, and have the oneness. Do not think that in the Gospel of John there is no commission for gospel preaching. This book does have the commission for gospel preaching, but it has it in another way, not in the way of activity, movement, work, or crusade, but in the way of a life always under the pruning of the heavenly Husbandman, always abiding in the Son of God, always praying for certain persons to be brought into the reality of the increase of Christ, and always loving the brothers regardless of their condition or situation. We simply love the brothers because of the Lord Christ. We have learned the lessons and are being built up together with them. This is the prevailing power, the convincing life, of gospel preaching. The gospel preaching is the increase of Christ, and this increase can be possible only by our being put to death. We must learn the lessons from John 15 and 17. How much we need to be built up!

## PREACHING THE GOSPEL IN THE WAY OF LIFE
## FOR THE INCREASE OF CHRIST

We are now in the process of the Lord's recovery. I would ask you, honestly and humbly, to be patient with the building up. We have been tested by our gospel preaching as to where we are, and now we have to be built up. Do not take any concept from your background of Christianity. I say this humbly and honestly. We have been too influenced by that, and we are still under that influence. The proper outreach of the gospel is not a kind of movement, and it is not a kind of crusade. It is a life that is crucified, pruned, abiding in Christ, and being built up. This requires more time. Then we will see the prevailing preaching.

Do not expect, according to your old concept, that we are preparing to have a work of gospel preaching and that suddenly in one night the results will come. That is just a dream. For many years we have seen reports concerning the gospel with numbers in black and white, but where is the real result? Where are the people today? Where is the real fruit? Do we want to follow that way? In the Gospel of life the way to produce fruit, the way to have Christ increased, is the way of life.

I do not want to say too much about the churches in the Far East. We have seen, though, that they have no need for a crusade or gospel preaching movement. The saints in Taipei simply have a life for the gospel, and monthly and yearly a number of people are brought into the increase of Christ. This is because they have the building up. We need the patience to be built up, and this building up is revealed in all of the steps we have fellowshipped about. No doubt, we already have the divine birth, but what about the growth? What about drinking the Lord and feeding upon Him? And what about maturity and the building up? We have to humble ourselves and see the proper way.

Many things which we have seen in our background of Christianity are not accurate. They are more or less distracting. I beg you to learn the lesson to drop those things and come back to the Lord and to the way of life. Read the Gospel of John once again. In the first three Gospels—Matthew, Mark, and Luke—there is the commission for gospel preaching, seemingly in a way of activity. In the last Gospel, however, the Gospel of life, this commission is not mentioned in the way of activity but in the way of life. Without the way of life, we can bring people to Christ only in an outward way; we cannot see Christ increased. In order to have Christ increased with persons, we must live a crucified life, imparting Christ all the time, not merely bringing people to Christ, but imparting Christ to people, transforming people into the parts of the bride of Christ.

I look to the Lord that in these days we all may be helped by the Holy Spirit to see that the proper outreach of the gospel is the imparting of Christ to others. This requires our abiding in Him and our being pruned, purged, and broken, that is, our being crucified. Then something of Christ will grow out of and through all of us. Christ will be imparted into others. We will have the real increase, and this increase is the bride of Christ. This is the proper preaching of the gospel. This is the outreach of the gospel in the way of life.

CHAPTER TWELVE

## PREACHING THE GOSPEL ACCORDING TO THE MENDING MINISTRY OF JOHN

Scripture Reading: John 10:10b; 3:29-30; 12:24-26; 15:4-5; 17:21

The writings of the apostle John are classified into three groups. The first is his Gospel, the second group is his Epistles, and the last is the book of Revelation. It is very interesting that in the arrangement of the order of the New Testament books, all the writings of John are put at the end of each category. This is not because these books were the last books written; in this case they would all be at the end of the New Testament. Under the sovereignty of the Lord, the arrangement of the New Testament books is not chronological. Rather, John's Gospel is at the end of the Gospels, and his Epistles are at the end of the Epistles. Even after Jude there are the seven epistles in the book of Revelation, which is at the end of the entire New Testament. The reason for this is very meaningful. We can see the real sovereignty of the Lord concerning the Bible.

John's ministry is not the ministry for starting but the ministry for completing. His ministry is not the fishing ministry that brings people in; it is the mending ministry to keep people in the testimony by mending the work of the Lord. If we take this point of view and study all the books of this apostle in this way, we will have new light.

At the end of the Gospel of Matthew, the Lord Jesus says, "Go therefore and disciple all the nations, baptizing them into the name of the Father and of the Son and of the Holy Spirit" (28:19). In Mark the Lord Jesus said almost the same thing: "Go into all the world and proclaim the gospel to all the creation" (16:15), and in Luke there is a similar word (24:47-49).

The endings of these first three Gospels tell us the same thing—that we have to go, preach the gospel to all the nations and to all creation, and disciple the Gentiles. When we come to the last Gospel, however, we do not have this kind of word or commandment. The Lord's commission in the Gospel of John is not in this way. In John we have the way to preach the gospel in and by life, the way to preach the gospel by the mending ministry.

The history of the church, our own experiences, and the present situation of Christianity all prove that if we do not have the way mentioned and revealed in this Gospel, if we have only the way revealed in the first three Gospels, the preaching of the gospel will not have a prevailing result. The result of the preaching of the gospel is kept by the way of life revealed in the Gospel of John. If we do not know the way to preach the gospel revealed in this book, and we only know the way mentioned in the first three books, the result of our preaching will leak away, because there will be nothing to mend and keep the result.

It is very easy for Christians to realize the way of preaching the gospel that is mentioned in the first three Gospels. This is because even though that way is not, strictly speaking, out of the human concept, it is similar to the human concept. The way to preach the gospel by life and in life, however, as revealed in the Gospel of John, requires heavenly revelation and spiritual insight. Otherwise, we cannot see it; it will seem that in this Gospel the Lord never says anything about the preaching of His gospel. The Lord did speak of the gospel, but He spoke in the way of life, not in the way that the natural concept can apprehend.

We still need the way revealed in the first three Gospels. We have to go, and we have to preach. However, if we do not have the way of life, whatever we reap with one hand, we will lose with the other hand. We may compare this to bringing water out of a well and putting it into a leaking basin. We need something to keep and contain what we have.

Consider the history of the church and the present situation of Christianity. Many people have been brought to the Lord through campaigns and crusades, but where are they now? We cannot account for them, because Christianity today mostly uses the way spoken of in the first three Gospels and neglects the way in the Gospel of John. It uses the fishing way while neglecting the mending way. Some people were brought to the Lord through me thirty-five years ago, but at that time I did not know this mending way. Now I do not know where many of them are. They truly came to the Lord, but eventually they leaked away. Only a few, who have been truly helped by the mending ministry, the ministry of life, are still in the church life.

While we do acknowledge the first way of preaching, we have to pay our full attention to the second way, the way of life, the way of Christ increased through us. For the long run, the best and proper way for the church and the members of the church to preach the gospel is the way of life. We all have to learn this way, and we have to pay attention to this way.

It is easy for us to apprehend the first way because it is very close to our natural concept. However, to apprehend the second way to preach the gospel, the way of life, we need revelation. We need spiritual insight to see that the way to preach the gospel is to impart Christ to others. This is for Christ to be increased through us and into others. Therefore, there is the absolute need of life. We must have this life. If we do not have this life, we cannot impart Christ to others. Even in the physical life, we cannot expect a person who is childish, weak, or ill to impart life to others. There is the need of the real growth in life; then life can be imparted to others. In order to preach the gospel in the way of life, we have to grow. If a branch of a tree has no growth and is poor in life, how can it bear fruit? If we are going to bear fruit for the increase of Christ through us, we must have life abundantly. The Lord Jesus said, "I have come that they may have life and may have it abundantly" (John 10:10b). To have life is good for ourselves, but if we are going to impart life to others, we must have life abundantly. Therefore, we need to grow.

## LEARNING TO CARE FOR PEOPLE THROUGH THE GOSPEL

If we are truly growing and have growth, we need to practice at least four things. First, we must care for the unbelievers. Regardless of how spiritual we are and what kind of spiritual attainment we have made, even if we are as experienced as the apostle Paul, we still need to care for people by preaching the gospel. Brother Watchman Nee gathered one hundred forty-seven names within one and a half years. He constantly prayed for these names. We all have to practice this. We have to go to the Lord to consider all the people surrounding us— relatives, neighbors, friends, schoolmates, colleagues, and others, not only the people whom we know locally but also those we know who are far away. If someone is far off, we still need to bear the burden for him. We should fellowship with the Lord. Then He will lead us to take care of certain ones. This is something for the long run. We must not expect to bring people to the Lord too quickly. Rather, we have to pray for them daily. This requires a real fellowship with the Lord.

In order to pray, we ourselves have to be dealt with. If we have a separation from the Lord, we will be hindered. We will not be able to pray with a pure conscience, and we will not have the boldness, the assurance, and the faith that our prayer can be answered. Therefore, we need to be dealt with. If we mean business with the Lord to care for others, we will constantly be dealt with by the Lord. This will help us to grow. The more we are willing to be dealt with by the Lord, the more we will grow, and the more we grow, the more we will have the abundant life to share with others.

We must practice to pray. We do not want to give the impression that we are legalistic or formal, but in some places the saints, especially the young ones, made the decision to pray for at least five people. I do not want to make a regulation of this, but we practiced this way when we were young. When I was younger, I always carried some tracts in my pocket. At that time I walked for thirty minutes to the office where I worked. As I was walking, I would always pass the tracts out to every kind of person I met, and if there was the time, I would talk to a few people.

When the Lord first began the work in my hometown, I was by myself. One evening a friend of mine came to talk with me about a certain matter. Before that time, we had both been members of the Chinese Independent Church, where, being about ten years older than I, he was one of the elders. Because that was in July, the hot time of the year, I suggested that we go to the beach to have a time of fellowship. As we sat on the sand, he asked me about various matters, such as baptism and the Lord's table. After two or three hours, I suggested we go back home. Instead, he wanted to remain, and he asked me to baptize him. That was the beginning of the work there. I baptized him even though I was simply a layman, a young person, not a pastor, preacher, elder, or deacon. We two were in the heavens. He said to me, "Mr. Lee, from tonight I will drop the Chinese Independent Church. Let us two pray together and read the Bible." I agreed to this.

On the third day afterward, I asked one of my office colleagues concerning that person. He wanted to know why I was asking, so I said, "I will tell you a secret. The day before yesterday, I baptized him in the sea." Right away he said, "Mr. Lee, this afternoon after work you have to baptize me." This man had been saved through me. I told him to wait a little, because there was another man who was saved who might also want to be baptized. A few minutes later that other person came, and we checked with him. He said, "I am willing. Let us do it." So on that day another two were baptized. Then we were four. That was a Thursday, and by the next Lord's Day, we had eleven people. We were like the early disciples, just eleven brothers meeting together to have the Lord's table. After that, the Lord sent more people to us.

The principle here is that the Lord will send people to us if we have a real testimony in life. We all have to learn the lesson to care for others. We have to pray for certain names and make this kind of preaching a part of our life. We are living here for this. This is not merely our work or activity; this is a part of our life. I can testify that it is altogether true that if we pray for others, sooner or later they will be saved. It takes time. Learn to bear this burden.

In the past twenty-five years, I saw a good number of spiritual persons. However, they went to an extreme. The more they became spiritual, the more they neglected this kind of preaching. That is one hundred percent wrong. We need the balance of preaching with spirituality. The more we become spiritual, the more we have to bear the burden of preaching. This is the first thing we have to practice.

## HAVING A TESTIMONY IN LIFE

Second, along with our prayer and preaching, we must have a testimony in life. Without a testimony in life, our preaching and prayer will not be prevailing. A person once preached the gospel to his colleagues for more than ten years. Day by day he did the preaching but without result. This is because he had no testimony in life. On the one hand, he passed out tracts and preached the gospel, but on the other hand, he argued with people and easily lost his temper. That spoiled and hindered his preaching. There is the need of a testimony in life. We have to fall into the earth to die for Jesus' sake, and we must be resurrected. Then we will have a testimony in our daily life.

## The Testimony of a Humble Employee

I can never forget a certain brother who studied engineering in this country. After graduation he went back to China, and by the time I met him, he was the head of a department in our college. I was surprised that such a highly educated and high ranking person could be saved. He told me his story, which was very inspiring. For several years a certain brother worked under him in the government. This brother held a very low position. In China, especially in the early years, people in high positions looked down on those in positions like this. They considered them unequal to themselves and did not like even to talk to them. However that brother, a lowly, small employee in that department, tried his best to contact the head of the department and tell him about the Lord Jesus. The head considered that since he had studied in America, he knew all about Christianity, and he did not need it. It seemed that the lowly brother could do nothing, but every morning he came early to the office and put a tract on the desk of the department head. When that man came in, he saw it. This happened every day without exception for several years.

That man was not happy with the brother, but he could not

fire him. After about three to five years, the man spoke with his wife, who had also studied in America. He said, "Let us go to that poor fellow's home and see what they are and what they are doing." That he suddenly had such a thought must have been the Lord's answer to prayer. The couple went to visit the brother. They went into his home and stayed for a certain time. The testimony was there. They noticed their family life and were impressed. After they returned home, they talked with each other. The man said, "We two are highly educated. You studied home economics, but how poor our home is. Those people are from a lower class. They have not been educated as we have been, but what a wonderful family life they have!" This was the brother's testimony.

That couple again contacted the poor brother and his wife and asked them how they had such a beautiful family life. The brother's answer was simply that they had Jesus. At this point the Holy Spirit convinced them. This highly educated couple in the highest position knelt down, prayed, and accepted the Lord, and they were saved. Not long after that, I was invited to their town, and I stayed in their home. They truly loved the Lord. They were saved through preaching in the way of life. That was not only the preaching of the gospel; that was the imparting of life, the imparting of Christ. This is the increase of Christ.

I was also invited to the first brother's home. He gave me the testimony with tears of how much he suffered just for that one couple. He was despised, looked down upon, and treated poorly because that man was in the higher position. The department head was not happy with this poor brother, so he did many things to persecute him, and the little brother suffered all the time. Still, whenever he saw that high official, he always smiled at him humbly. Regardless of how he was treated, he was happy within and put a tract on his desk over a period of several years, even though all the tracts, without exception, went into the wastebasket. I have heard many such stories as this one.

## The Testimony of a Missionary

The first Presbyterian missionaries who went to China

had a real love toward those poor Gentiles, and they had a testimony. That love and testimony convinced the people, and through that, the door for the gospel was opened. Otherwise, it would have been too hard to open the door among the poor, conservative Chinese. One story is the most inspiring. At that time, no doors for the gospel were open. The missionaries could not do anything. The people made a corporate decision that no one in the whole village would open his door to any of the foreign missionaries. Whenever a foreign missionary came to the village, a gong was beaten to warn of his coming. Then all the people closed their doors. Not one person in the whole village would come out of his home until the gong was sounded again because the missionary was gone.

One dear brother, who was a missionary, studied the situation and began to pray. The people would close their entrances and wait for a long time. The brother would stand beside a door, and when someone would open it to see if the foreigner had gone, the brother would put a stick into the door. He would push the door until he was half through it, and then regardless of what the people inside did, he would push all the way through. In China in the early days, almost every home had a grinding room with a millstone to grind the wheat and corn. That was a hard task since there was no power in those homes. If someone was rich, he would use a horse or mule to do the work, but if he was poor, he would do the grinding by himself.

The missionary studied this situation. After coming through a door, he would right away run to the mill to do the grinding work for the people. The whole family would pay no attention to that poor fellow. They said, "If he is willing to do the hard work for us, let him do it." The brother would continue to grind without stopping for several hours, almost for the whole day. That touched the heart of the people in the family, especially the older generation. The grandfather would come and give him a cup of water and say, "Drink it." The missionary would thank him and drink it. Then he would keep on grinding. That truly touched them. It was because of this that the older generation was opened to the brother. They would say, "Please sit down and have a rest. How old are you?

From where did you come?" It was through this that the doors were opened one by one.

There are other such stories that are truly inspiring. I would impress you that there is no easy way to bear fruit. If a grain of wheat is to bear fruit, it has to fall into the earth, die, and be resurrected. Then the life will come out. Almost everyone, especially in this country, knows something about Christianity. We cannot win people in a light way or easy way. Rather, we have to pay the price. We have to win people at a certain cost. We have to pay a price for our relatives, neighbors, colleagues, and classmates. We must pray for them and testify the Lord Jesus to them, giving them a real testimony in life.

There is the need of a testimony in life. This kind of testimony cannot be built up in one or two days. It requires a certain period of time. As students in school, we have to build up a testimony day by day. Then after a few weeks or months the way will be prepared to bring people to the Lord. This is the most prevailing way. In this way, not only will people be brought to the Lord, but they will also be kept. I say again, this is not merely the preaching of the gospel but also the imparting of life to others. We have to practice this. In order to be balanced, we must have a life of preaching.

## BEING BUILT UP AS LIVING MEMBERS
## OF THE BODY OF CHRIST

The third thing we must practice is to be built up. We must be able to show to the whole universe, especially to those for whom we are concerned, that we are living members of the Body of Christ. To do this, we should invite the brothers and sisters who are built together with us to help us deal with the unbelievers. If we are not built up together, it is hard to invite brothers to share the preaching with us. Even if we do invite someone, there will be no impact and vitality. If, however, we are built together in love, people will be able to sense it. When we invite the brothers and sisters to help us deal with the unbelievers, they will sense that there is something among us. They will sense the love and that there is something wonderful among us. This is very convincing to people. This kind of building up and oneness paves the way for the Holy Spirit to work something into the unbelievers. If we do not have the oneness, however, even if we all come together, there will be no impact. Satan will laugh at us, and the Holy Spirit will be choked. There will be no way for the Holy Spirit to work something of Christ into people. There is the need of the oneness, the building up.

When we are built up together, it is effective to invite unbelievers to come to our meeting. The meeting of built-up Christians is very prevailing. However, if we are not built up together and we are loose in coming together, there will be no impact. In the early 1940s in my hometown, people were very impressed by our meetings. In their common talk they would say to each other that anyone who went to those meetings would be convinced. There was an impact there.

In the same way, many people who have come to our meetings here were also very impressed. They can forget the message, but they cannot forget the meeting and the atmosphere in the meeting. There is the oneness and the living impact. Suppose, on the other hand, that we are not built up with one another. When we come to the meeting, we come unhappy and disappointed with the brothers. Then when one brother chooses a hymn, someone else just shakes his head, and we sing it in a poor way. In this case, there is no impact. However, suppose that we are built together as one in love. Whenever we come together, we love one another. All the brothers and sisters are happy to see one another, and we feel that it is wonderful to be together. In this case, the Spirit will be released. Whatever hymn anyone calls, we simply sing it right away in the spirit, in love, and in oneness. That kind of meeting will be very convincing.

One brother who came to our meetings went back and told people, "Oh, you do not know what kind of meeting that was! When you come into the meeting, their singing, the oneness, and the anointing are wonderful. The anointing within me kept telling me that this is the answer." He was impressed in this way not by hearing a message but simply by attending the meeting. Then he asked as many people as he could to come to our conference here. He wanted them to come just to hear our singing. Some who came to our first meeting for the preaching of the gospel went back to their city and reported that heaven came down in that meeting. I have heard many things like this.

We must learn to love the Lord, fellowship with Him, live by Him, and walk in Him, and we must learn how to exercise our spirit to contact the Lord and release Him from our spirit. We must also pray for the sinners, preach the gospel to them, have the testimony of life, come together in love, and be truly built up. Then whenever we come together there will be the impact. This is the proper and only way to testify the Lord. Other things may be a help, but they are not the main, proper way. The proper way is this kind of life, including the church life.

The unbelievers who are brought into the church life through this way of life will be kept in life. The life will constantly mend and keep them. This life will become the keeping power. The most prevailing way to preach the gospel is the way of life and the way of the Body life. We must not neglect the practical way we come together, but we cannot pretend. If we do not love one another and do not have a daily life in Christ through the Spirit, we may pretend that we have something when we come together. However, the Holy Spirit will never testify to this, and the evil one will laugh at us, regardless of what way we meet. There must be a life as our backing. We must have this life in our daily walk, and we must be truly built up and love one another. Then whenever we come together, we will have the reality, the backing. We will have the atmosphere, the singing in the spirit, the release of the Spirit, and the proper prayer. This will convince people. This is the "warm climate" to warm people up. It is not a matter of teaching, doctrine, or preaching. Many times people are not infused by the teachings, but it is always easy for people to be influenced and convinced by a certain kind of feeling and atmosphere. If we have such a meeting in oneness and in life, full of love and the release of the spirit, this kind of meeting will impress people.

In our hometown an unbeliever was saved in a wedding meeting. This woman did not know the brothers or sisters.

She simply was standing on the street and noticed that a meeting was going on. She was a complete Gentile and had never heard the gospel. She came in to sit and watch the wedding. Actually, that was not merely a wedding; it was a Christian meeting full of the Holy Spirit. The singing and the love were inspiring. On that day she said to herself, "I have to find out what kind of people these are. What are they doing here?" In this way, this woman, a widow, was easily saved. In that meeting there was no gospel preaching; it was just a wedding meeting. Even through such a wedding meeting, however, this woman was saved simply by the atmosphere, which was sweet, full of love, and inspiring.

Even if people cannot understand in their mentality, still their heart and spirit can sense that there is something sweet and convincing here. We need to have such a meeting. This depends on our oneness and our being built up. In this oneness and building there is love, humility, kindness, meekness, and all good things. It is through this oneness that the Holy Spirit is released and the enemy is subdued. Then people are convinced. It is so easy. Moreover, people who are brought into the church life in this way will always be kept by this mending and keeping life.

## CONTACTING PEOPLE BY EXERCISING THE SPIRIT

The fourth thing we must practice is always to contact people by exercising the spirit. It is too easy to preach by arguing. We should forget about this kind of preaching and forget about arguing. Before one elderly brother among us was saved, he asked Brother Watchman Nee many questions, but Brother Nee did not answer. Brother Nee simply exercised his spirit to ask him one question: "Did you commit sin?" Do not deal with people's mentality but with their conscience, their spirit. We can only touch people's spirit by exercising our spirit. If we exercise our mind, we can only touch people's mind. Therefore, we need to live and have our daily walk by exercising our spirit. Then we will know how to exercise our spirit. We will be accustomed to it, and whenever we contact people, we will not pay much attention to talking, preaching, or arguing. We will pay attention to dealing with their spirit.

If we learn how to exercise in this way, we will pave the way for the Holy Spirit to do many things.

All the foregoing matters are not mere teachings. I do not want to have more teachings. Rather, we need to know, experience, and practice many things. If we would practice the above four matters, we will learn much, not by being taught but by practicing. We must care for others and pray for them, bear the burden, have a life as a real testimony, be built up with others, and learn to exercise the spirit. Then we will be very productive. In a gradual way, monthly and yearly, people will be brought to the Lord. This preaching is not merely a preaching. It is the real increase of Christ. We will see the branches of the vine become fruitful, and the church life will be built up. This is what we need. We must consider this kind of preaching as a part of our human life. We look to the Lord for His strengthening and His help in this regard.

# CHAPTER THIRTEEN

## BEARING THE RESPONSIBILITY
## TO FEED SPIRITUAL CHILDREN

Scripture Reading: John 21:14-17; S. S. 1:2-8

In this message we will consider the last chapter of the Gospel of John and the first chapter of the Song of Songs. The order of the writings in the Bible is very meaningful. According to the human concept, we would never imagine that there would be a story of shepherding at the end of John, the Gospel of life. John 21:14 says, "This was now the third time that Jesus was manifested to the disciples after He had been raised from the dead." Note that here the Lord calls them His disciples, not apostles. In this context, we should not consider Peter as an apostle. Peter is not in the position of an apostle but on the ground of a disciple when the Lord deals with him. Therefore, what follows is something related to the disciples.

### FEEDING ON THE LORD
### AND FEEDING HIS LAMBS

Verses 15 through 17 continue, "Then when they had eaten breakfast, Jesus said to Simon Peter, Simon, son of John, do you love Me more than these? He said to Him, Yes, Lord, You know that I love You. He said to him, Feed My lambs. He said to him again a second time, Simon, son of John, do you love Me? He said to Him, Yes, Lord, You know that I love You. He said to him, Shepherd My sheep. He said to him the third time, Simon, son of John, do you love Me? Peter was grieved that He said to him the third time, Do you love Me? And he said to Him, Lord, You know all things; You know that I love

You. Jesus said to him, Feed My sheep." Notice that twice the Lord used the same word, *feed*.

As we have seen, the first section of the Gospel of John, in chapters one through three, deals with the birth of life. The second section, starting from chapter four, deals with the growth of life, and the third section is on the maturity of life, which is the building up. The more we read this book and get into it, the more we will see that this is the right order. The birth of life is a matter by the spirit and of the spirit: "That which is born of the Spirit is spirit" (3:6b). Growth is a matter of eating and drinking. In John 4, drinking comes before eating, because drinking is more fundamental than eating. Then in chapter six there is the eating, and in chapter seven there is drinking again. This is the way we take a meal; we drink something first, then we eat, and then after eating we drink again. Drinking and eating, eating and drinking, are for the growth.

The last section, especially from chapter ten and onward, is for the maturity of life, that is, for the building up. The important word in chapter seventeen is *one*. Verse 21 says, "That they all may be one; even as You, Father, are in Me and I in You, that they also may be in Us; that the world may believe that You have sent Me." Oneness is the building up, and it is maturity. Until we are built up with others, we can never reach maturity. Being built up is a proof that we are mature. The birth of life is a matter of the spirit, growth is a matter of drinking and eating, and maturity is a matter of oneness.

At the end of the Gospel of John there is the record of how the Lord Jesus told Peter to feed His sheep. All Bible students who know this book agree that chapter twenty-one is a "postscript." After someone writes a letter, he may add something as a "P.S." at the end to make the letter more clear. The end of chapter twenty says, "Moreover indeed many other signs also Jesus did before His disciples, which are not written in this book. But these have been written that you may believe that Jesus is the Christ, the Son of God, and that believing, you may have life in His name" (vv. 30-31). Seemingly, at the end of the twentieth chapter, the book of John concludes. After this conclusion, however, there is another chapter, chapter twenty-one as a postscript.

Both the composition and the meaning of chapter twenty-one give us the same impression that even if we know the Lord as life, grow in Him, and are built up, there is one thing that still is easy to neglect. We know we need to grow, to pay our full attention to growth, and we have seen the light that we have to be built up. However, we must realize that as we are growing and being built up, we need to be balanced and feed others. While we are feeding on the Lord, we have to feed others. We have to feed the lambs. We must be like mothers, who feed on their own food and then feed their children. If there were not such a chapter as John 21, we may easily neglect taking care of and feeding others.

As we have seen, the Gospel of John is not like the other three Gospels. At the end of the other three Gospels, there is the commandment, the so-called great commission, from the Lord to go and preach the gospel. It seems, though, that there is no such commission in this book. However, this book says, "Feed My lambs....Feed My sheep." Firstly the Lord tells us to feed on Him, and then He says to feed others. This is the balance. Regardless of how spiritual we are, how much growth we have, and how much we have been built up, if we are not feeding others all the time, we are wrong; we are out of balance. Under the Lord's sovereignty there are some spiritual children that we need to take care of.

### SEEKING THE LORD
### AND PASTURING THE YOUNG GOATS

In the Song of Songs there is a seeking one, representing a believer who not only is saved but to some degree is trained and dealt with by the Lord. Song of Songs 1:2a says, "Let him kiss me with the kisses of his mouth!" For the Lord to kiss us is for Him to show His love to us. After asking the Lord to show His love, the seeking one immediately realizes His love and says, "For your love is better than wine. / Your anointing oils have a pleasant fragrance; / Your name is like ointment poured forth; / Therefore the virgins love you. / Draw me; we will run after you— / The king has brought me into his chambers— / We will be glad and rejoice in you; / We will extol your love more than wine. / Rightly do they love you" (vv. 2b-4). If we ourselves are drawn by the Lord, then others also will run after Him.

Verses 5 and 6 continue, "I am black but lovely, O daughters of Jerusalem, / Like the tents of Kedar, like the curtains of Solomon. / Do not look at me, because I am black, / Because the sun has scorched me. / My mother's sons were angry with me; / They made me keeper of the vineyards, / But my own vineyard I have not kept." At this point, the seeker realizes two things. First, in the past she was forced to take care of other vineyards, but she did not care for her own. That means that she did many other things, but she neglected her own life condition. Now she realizes her shortage. She has to take care of her own condition, her own inner life. Second, she is hungry and has no satisfaction. Therefore, she prays, "Tell me, you whom my soul loves, / Where do you pasture your flock? / Where do you make it lie down at noon? / For why should I be like one who is veiled / Beside the flocks of your companions?" (v. 7). She realizes that she needs feeding, satisfaction, and rest, and she wants to know where to find it. The Lord answers her, "If you yourself do not know, / You fairest among women, / Go forth on the footsteps of the flock, / And pasture your young goats / By the shepherds' tents" (v. 8). To follow the footsteps of the flock is to follow the church. If she follows the flock, the church, she will find the place where the Lord feeds His young goats.

In the Lord's answer there is a balance. While we seek to feed on the Lord, we have to feed others. We have to take care of our "young goats." We should not think, "Formerly I worked too much. Now I will forget about that and pay my full attention to seeking the Lord to satisfy myself. I am hungry, and I am thirsty. I have no rest. Lord, let me know where You feed Your flock, where You give Your flock rest, that I may be satisfied and have rest." On the one hand, this is right. On the other hand, though, while we are seeking the Lord, we have to be balanced. We must not forget our "young goats." If we do not have spiritual children, we are wrong; we have to bring forth some children.

## OUR NEED FOR SPIRITUAL CHILDREN

The young brothers and sisters need children to balance them. All the young fathers and mothers learn the best lessons from their children. If someone does not have children, he is not balanced. We neglect this too much. It is a real problem that there are many dear ones among us, but not many have spiritual children. Even according to the flesh, if the brothers and sisters do not have children, there is something seriously wrong. The more children we have, the more we are right. Someone may argue with this, but I assure you that the Lord stands with me in saying it. In Genesis 1 the Lord told Adam to fill the earth with children (v. 28). The earth is not yet filled up. The earth has to be filled. Without children, how can the Lord's purpose be fulfilled? How can He have the material to fulfill His eternal purpose? Do not be afraid of having a big family. The bigger a family is, the better. To have a family without children means we are wrong in some way.

In the church there must be many spiritual children, the more the better. When we come to the meeting, we should come with three or four spiritual children, one on the right, one on the left, one at the back, and one in the front. That would be wonderful. In this case, we will have the real growth.

All the young mothers and fathers learn the real lessons of human life by having children. When I was young, close to thirty years ago, by the mercy of the Lord I already had two or three children. At the same time there were a number of sisters in the church, many of whom were nurses. Those sisters were trained and very capable. When they went to the homes of the brothers and sisters who had children, they did not criticize outwardly, but they criticized inwardly very much. I knew this because a number of times they came to me and told me how they felt about certain sisters and brothers. I did not argue, but I said to myself, "All right, sisters, wait four or five years. You will have two children. Then I will go to your home and see how you manage it." I told them, "Wait for a time and see." They thought I meant that they should wait and see about those other families. They did not realize that I meant, "Wait and see how you will manage." Sometimes after a few months, one of those sisters would get married, and after two or three years she would have children. From then on her mouth was shut; she no longer criticized. If we have two or three spiritual children, we will learn the lessons. Our criticizing mouth will be shut, and our criticizing heart will be calmed down. Then we will know only to sympathize with others. It is not a small thing to take care of children.

Allow me to illustrate this further. When we were young, the sisters who came to our home liked our little babies, but if the babies dirtied their diapers, the sisters would quickly give them back to the mother. When those sisters married and had their own children, however, there was no way for them to give their children to someone else. They had to take care of the dirty diapers themselves. In this way they learned the lessons. If we do not have children under our care, we learn only one thing—to enjoy. Moreover, if we cannot have our enjoyment, spontaneously we criticize; we never sympathize. This is the case until one day we pick up the responsibility to take care of four or five, even ten or twenty children. Then our mouths will be shut, and our hearts will be calmed down. We will sympathize with others, we will realize our responsibility, and we will learn the lessons.

By the Lord's mercy, even physically speaking we had a number of children when we were young, and I learned certain lessons. Spiritually speaking also, even from my youth I had many spiritual children, and I learned more lessons. Now it is hard for me to criticize, but it is easy, by the Lord's mercy, to sympathize. Today if I go to a sisters' home where there are several children and there is some problem, I do not criticize; I only sympathize. Having children helps us to learn the lessons. As disciples, we all need to take care of some children.

### KNOWING HOW AND BEING ABLE TO FEED OTHERS

The main point in this message is the word *feed*. To feed is not to teach. We need something with which we can feed others, and we need to know the way to feed others. First we have to take care of some spiritual children, either some young believers, some new converts, or some unbelievers. Then we have to learn the lesson to prepare something to feed them with, and we have to learn the way to feed them.

It is not my intention merely to give some messages. Rather, this is a training. It is not enough to listen to these matters without practicing them. I beg you to put all these things into practice. From now on try to pick up a few spiritual children, and learn to feed them. Then you will see your shortage. Mothers learn by feeding their children. Whether someone knows the way of life and how to feed on the Lord Jesus will be tested by his feeding of others. Suppose that today we gain three spiritual children. We may not know how to feed them. We may say, "I have nothing to feed them." Then we will see that we are short of feeding. What we feed others must be the thing that we have taken in and digested, just as mothers feed their children with the things they have taken in and digested. This is not to teach but to feed.

I like the word *feed*. The Lord Jesus did not say, "Take care of My lambs"; He said, "Feed My lambs." Someone may say, "Now I am taking care of some young believers." However, to take care is one thing, but to feed is another. Some brothers truly love the Lord and love others, and they take care of others. However, they take care of them without feeding them. If a new, young convert loses his job, a brother may help him to get another job. This is to take care of him, but there may be no feeding. To feed people is more than to take care of them. It is a matter of life. We have to feed on the Lord ourselves; then we will digest something of the Lord and will have something from within with which we can feed others. To feed others is a matter of life, just as for mothers to feed their children is a matter of life, not of knowledge or anything else. This is why the account in John 21 is not recorded in chapters seventeen, fifteen, or twelve. Even by chapter twelve Peter was not qualified. He was too short of life. Feeding others requires a certain amount of life.

We all have to pay attention to this matter. If the church life is proper and normal, we all will take care of some spiritual children and continually feed them. I say again, if we would try to practice in this way, we will discover our shortages. We will see that we are short of many spiritual experiences. If you would make the decision to feed two or three spiritual children, after only two weeks you will discover your shortages; you will see what you are lacking. Then you will seek the Lord in a proper way that you may learn how to feed on the Lord and how to feed others.

## FEEDING OTHERS CAUSING
## OUR OWN PROBLEMS TO BE SOLVED

This is a matter of feeding, not merely a matter of teaching. If we expect the church and the saints to grow unto maturity, we all must learn the lesson to take care of some spiritual children and feed them all the time. Otherwise, there will be no real growth among us. We should not simply meet here year after year, not increasing by caring for spiritual children. The increase of the church must be in the way of taking care of the "young goats." If we do this, we will be right and balanced, and this will solve many problems.

It is too easy for young sisters and brothers who have no family and children to go to one another to "talk," that is, to gossip, under the good pretense of fellowshipping in the Lord. This is actually fellowshipping in the way of gossiping. In the past I saw this too much. I tried my best in certain local churches to help these saints not to contact each other in this way. I even gave messages telling them, "If you are going to visit a brother, you first have to pray. You have to consecrate yourself to the Lord and seek the Lord's guidance, and you need to have the anointing within. Otherwise, you should not go." Even though I gave strong messages about this, they did not have much effect. The young ones still had the stirring within them to gossip. This went on until those persons were married. Marriage is truly a bondage. The best way to be bound is to marry. After one year, one child came, and after two or three years, more children came. Then these sisters could no longer contact others to gossip. With three children, they did not have time even to sleep. When I saw this, I said, "Praise the Lord. Those children are better than my messages." If we have spiritual children, we will have only responsibility, not gossip. We will not have enough time even to sleep.

Everything will be exhausted by those children. This is good; praise the Lord for this!

In these few days I have exercised in my spirit to seek the Lord concerning what to speak in these messages. The Lord gave me the answer: "Tell them to have spiritual children. Then all their problems will be solved. The best way to solve their problems is to help them to have spiritual children. Then they will learn the lessons, and they will be able to avoid many negative things."

In some parts of this country, people do not like to have children, because children are naughty and noisy. However, if you are going to choose a neighborhood to live in, do not choose one that has no children. People who insist on not having children are the hardest people to deal with. They often come to complain that you play the piano too loud or that your radio is on too high. I would rather live with people who have many children. Then they can play their piano, and I can sing my hymn. They can march, and I can jump, and no one will complain. The way to solve the brothers' and sisters' problems is to help them to have spiritual children. All those who seek the Lord without feeding others are the ones who create problems. If someone is indifferent, the church can easily deal with him, but the more someone is seeking without feeding others, the more problems he creates. The right way for people to solve their problems is to have spiritual children. Then they will know where they are, and they will know what responsibility is. Moreover, they will know what the real growth in life and the experience of life are.

### FEEDING OTHERS HELPING THE CHURCH TO GROW IN LIFE AND BE BUILT UP

In this message I have only one burden, that is, to convince you that you need to feed others. Then you will see where you are and what you need. What you need is not a matter of knowledge, teaching, or anything else. What you need is a real experience of life, the real way to know how to feed on the Lord Jesus and experience something of Him. Then you also will know what other people need, and you will know what you have to minister to others, what you have to feed others with. Then you will be humbled, you will be calmed down, and you will become sympathetic with others who bear responsibility. This will help the church very much to grow and to be built up. I beg you to put this into practice. We truly need to pray for this. Let us all take the burden, the responsibility, not only to help others but to feed others, to feed some spiritual children. This truly involves growth and even maturity.

## ABOUT THE AUTHOR

Witness Lee was born in 1905 in northern China and raised in a Christian family. At age 19 he was fully captured for Christ and immediately consecrated himself to preach the gospel for the rest of his life. Early in his service, he met Watchman Nee, a renowned preacher, teacher, and writer. Witness Lee labored together with Watchman Nee under his direction. In 1934 Watchman Nee entrusted Witness Lee with the responsibility for his publication operation, called the Shanghai Gospel Bookroom.

Prior to the Communist takeover in 1949, Witness Lee was sent by Watchman Nee and his other co-workers to Taiwan to insure that the things delivered to them by the Lord would not be lost. Watchman Nee instructed Witness Lee to continue the former's publishing operation abroad as the Taiwan Gospel Bookroom, which has been publicly recognized as the publisher of Watchman Nee's works outside China. Witness Lee's work in Taiwan manifested the Lord's abundant blessing. From a mere 350 believers, newly fled from the mainland, the churches in Taiwan grew to 20,000 in five years.

In 1962 Witness Lee felt led of the Lord to come to the United States, settling in California. During his 35 years of service in the U.S., he ministered in weekly meetings and weekend conferences, delivering several thousand spoken messages. Much of his speaking has since been published as over 400 titles. Many of these have been translated into over fourteen languages. He gave his last public conference in February 1997 at the age of 91.

He leaves behind a prolific presentation of the truth in the Bible. His major work, *Life-study of the Bible,* comprises over 25,000 pages of commentary on every book of the Bible from the perspective of the believers' enjoyment and experience of God's divine life in Christ through the Holy Spirit. Witness Lee was the chief editor of a new translation of the New Testament into Chinese called the Recovery Version and directed the translation of the same into English. The Recovery Version also appears in a number of other languages. He provided an extensive body of footnotes, outlines, and spiritual cross references. A radio broadcast of his messages can be heard on Christian radio stations in the United States. In 1965 Witness Lee founded Living Stream Ministry, a non-profit corporation, located in Anaheim, California, which officially presents his and Watchman Nee's ministry.

Witness Lee's ministry emphasizes the experience of Christ as life and the practical oneness of the believers as the Body of Christ. Stressing the importance of attending to both these matters, he led the churches under his care to grow in Christian life and function. He was unbending in his conviction that God's goal is not narrow sectarianism but the Body of Christ. In time, believers began to meet simply as the church in their localities in response to this conviction. In recent years a number of new churches have been raised up in Russia and in many eastern European countries.

## Other Books Published By
### *Living Stream Ministry*

**Titles by Witness Lee:**

| | |
|---|---|
| Abraham—Called by God | 0-7363-0359-6 |
| The Experience of Life | 0-87083-417-7 |
| The Knowledge of Life | 0-87083-419-3 |
| The Tree of Life | 0-87083-300-6 |
| The Economy of God | 0-87083-415-0 |
| The Divine Economy | 0-87083-268-9 |
| God's New Testament Economy | 0-87083-199-2 |
| The World Situation and God's Move | 0-87083-092-9 |
| Christ vs. Religion | 0-87083-010-4 |
| The All-inclusive Christ | 0-87083-020-1 |
| Gospel Outlines | 0-87083-039-2 |
| Character | 0-87083-322-7 |
| The Secret of Experiencing Christ | 0-87083-227-1 |
| The Life and Way for the Practice of the Church Life | 0-87083-785-0 |
| The Basic Revelation in the Holy Scriptures | 0-87083-105-4 |
| The Crucial Revelation of Life in the Scriptures | 0-87083-372-3 |
| The Spirit with Our Spirit | 0-87083-798-2 |
| Christ as the Reality | 0-87083-047-3 |
| The Central Line of the Divine Revelation | 0-87083-960-8 |
| The Full Knowledge of the Word of God | 0-87083-289-1 |
| Watchman Nee—A Seer of the Divine Revelation ... | 0-87083-625-0 |

**Titles by Watchman Nee:**

| | |
|---|---|
| How to Study the Bible | 0-7363-0407-X |
| God's Overcomers | 0-7363-0433-9 |
| The New Covenant | 0-7363-0088-0 |
| The Spiritual Man    3 volumes | 0-7363-0269-7 |
| Authority and Submission | 0-7363-0185-2 |
| The Overcoming Life | 1-57593-817-0 |
| The Glorious Church | 0-87083-745-1 |
| The Prayer Ministry of the Church | 0-87083-860-1 |
| The Breaking of the Outer Man and the Release ... | 1-57593-955-X |
| The Mystery of Christ | 1-57593-954-1 |
| The God of Abraham, Isaac, and Jacob | 0-87083-932-2 |
| The Song of Songs | 0-87083-872-5 |
| The Gospel of God    2 volumes | 1-57593-953-3 |
| The Normal Christian Church Life | 0-87083-027-9 |
| The Character of the Lord's Worker | 1-57593-322-5 |
| The Normal Christian Faith | 0-87083-748-6 |
| Watchman Nee's Testimony | 0-87083-051-1 |

*Available at*
Christian bookstores, or contact Living Stream Ministry
2431 W. La Palma Ave. • Anaheim, CA 92801
1-800-549-5164 • www.livingstream.com